21 DAY DEVOTION

IDENTITY REVOLUTION

DISCOVER WHO YOU ARE

JASON HANASH

Discover Who You Are

Copyright © 2024 by Jason Hanash

All rights reserved. No portion of this book may be reproduced, stored in a retrieval system, or transmitted in any form or by any means—electronic, mechanical, photocopying, recording, scanning, or other—except for brief quotations in critical reviews or articles, without prior written permission of the author. Unless otherwise noted, all Scripture quotations are taken from the Holy Bible, New International Version®, NIV®. Copyright © 1973, 1978, 1984, 2011 by Biblica, Inc.™ Used by permission of Zondervan. All rights reserved worldwide. www.zondervan.com. The "NIV" and "New International Version" are trademarks registered in the United States Patent and Trademark Office by Biblica, Inc.™ Scripture quotations marked AMP are taken from the Amplified® Bible (AMP), Copyright © 2015 by The Lockman Foundation. Used by permission. www.lockman.org. Scripture quotations marked CEV are from the Contemporary English Version Copyright © 1995 by American Bible Society. Used by Permission. Scripture quotations marked ESV are from the ESV® Bible (The Holy Bible, English Standard Version®), copyright © 2001 by Crossway, a publishing ministry of Good News Publishers. Used by permission. All rights reserved. Scripture quotations marked GNT are from the Good News Translation in Today's English Version—Second Edition Copyright © 1992 by American Bible Society. Used by Permission. Scripture quotations marked MSG are taken from THE MESSAGE, copyright © 1993, 1994, 1995, 1996, 2000, 2001, 2002 by Eugene H. Peterson. Used by permission of NavPress. All rights reserved. Represented by Tyndale House Publishers, Inc. Scripture quotations marked NKJV are taken from the New King James Version®. Copyright © 1982 by Thomas Nelson. Used by permission. All rights reserved. Scripture quotations marked NLT are taken from the Holy Bible, New Living Translation, copyright © 1996, 2004, 2015 by Tyndale House Foundation. Used by permission of Tyndale House Publishers, Inc., Carol Stream, Illinois 60188. All rights reserved.

For foreign and subsidiary rights, contact the author.

Cover design by: Fabian Reyes
Cover photo by: Fabian Reyes
ISBN: 9798300679903
Printed in the United States of America

Dedication

To Veronica, my love and unwavering partner—your strength, faith, and constant belief in me have been a reflection of God's love in my life. This journey—not just of this book, but of my life—would not have been possible without you.

Table of Contents

The Identity Revolution 1
Chapter 1: The War for Your Identity 8
Chapter 2: Mirrors and Masks – The Image We Reflect 24
Chapter 3: Gender and the Gift of Identity 38
Chapter 4: Scrolling and Searching for Self 56
Chapter 5: The Father Gap – Finding Identity in a World of Absence ... 72

21 Day Devotion

Day 1: Created in God's Image 91
Day 2: New Creation in Christ 100
Day 3: Children of God 108
Day 4: Ambassadors of Christ 116
Day 5: Chosen and Royal Priesthood 124
Day 6: God's Masterpiece 132
Day 7: Co-Heirs with Christ 140
Day 8: Citizens of Heaven 148
Day 9: Salt and Light 155
Day 10: Temple of the Holy Spirit 163
Day 11: Set Free in Christ 171
Day 12: Branches of the True Vine 178
Day 13: Overcomers Through Christ 185
Day 14: Friends of God 193
Day 15: Loved by God 201
Day 16: Forgiven 209
Day 17: Holy and Blameless 217
Day 18: Part of the Body of Christ 225
Day 19: Victorious in Christ 233
Day 20: Alive in Christ 241
Day 21: Adopted into God's Family 248

The Identity Revolution
Catching God's Vision for a Generation

We are standing on the brink of a profound movement—a revolution that will transform the hearts and minds of a generation. This is more than just a shift in thinking; it's a seismic change that will redefine how we see ourselves, how we live, and how we walk in our God-given purpose. An Identity Revolution is coming, and it will shake the very foundations of our culture, leading us back to who God has created us to be.

Throughout history, the Church has experienced pivotal revolutions—moments where God broke through the noise of culture to ignite a movement that forever changed the trajectory of His people. These revolutions were not just religious awakenings; they were supernatural breakthroughs that reshaped entire societies.

Now, we stand on the threshold of a new revolution—an Identity Revolution that will capture the hearts of young adults and our youth, realigning their vision with the heart of God.

The Jesus Revolution

To understand the Identity Revolution that is coming, we must first look back at the revolutions that have shaped the Church. One of the most notable movements in recent history was the Jesus Revolution of the late 1960s and early 1970s. This was a time of cultural upheaval—war, political unrest, and widespread disillusionment with traditional institutions left young people searching for meaning and truth. It was a generation lost in the noise of the world, much like today.

In the midst of this chaos, God stirred the hearts of young people, igniting a revolution that brought radical transformation. The Jesus Movement was born not out of the traditional structures of the Church, but from a deep, desperate hunger for something real. Young people flocked to Jesus, shedding the trappings of the world for the simplicity and power of the Gospel. Lives were changed, and the ripple effect of this revolution can still be felt in the Church today.

What made the Jesus Revolution so powerful was that it spoke directly to the identity crisis of that generation. In a world that offered nothing but confusion, God offered clarity: You are loved, you are chosen, you are mine.

The Reformation

Before the Jesus Revolution, there was another groundbreaking shift—the Protestant Reformation of the 16th century. Led by figures like Martin Luther, this revolution came at a time when the

Church had become entangled in religious formalism, power, and corruption. People were spiritually starved, desperate for access to God's truth. The Reformation was not just a movement of reform; it was a revolution that restored the authority of Scripture and redefined the relationship between God and man.

The cultural climate was ripe for breakthrough—there was a growing hunger for truth, for freedom, for a return to the roots of faith. The Reformation shattered the barriers between people and God, declaring that we are saved by grace, not works, and that every believer is a priest in God's eyes. This revolution restored the core identity of the believer: We are saved, redeemed, and loved by a holy God.

Today's Climate: A Generation Under Siege

Today, we find ourselves in another moment of crisis. The enemy has launched an all-out assault on identity. From gender confusion to social media's distorted picture of self-worth, we are living in a time where identity has become one of the most contested battlegrounds. People are searching, longing for truth about who they are, but the world offers only shifting sand.

> **The culture promotes identities rooted in performance, appearance, and approval, but none of these can satisfy the soul.**

We see this struggle everywhere—from the rise in mental health issues to the deep divisions in our society.

The enemy's strategy is clear: If he can confuse people about who they are, he can derail them from their God-given purpose. But this is where the Identity Revolution begins.

I believe that we are on the verge of a supernatural awakening where sons and daughters will catch a vision for who they truly are in Christ.

> **This revolution will not be led by institutions, programs, or platforms—it will be fueled by a generation on fire for the truth of God's Word.**

Young men and women will rise up, declaring with boldness, *"I am who God says I am!"*

This Identity Revolution will tear down the lies of the enemy and replace them with the unshakable truth of God's Word:

- **You are made in His image.**
- **You are chosen.**
- **You are forgiven.**
- **You are victorious.**
- **You are part of God's family.**

In a world that says, "*You can be anything*," God says, "*You are Mine.*" This revolution will restore the truth that our identity is not in what we do, but in who we are in Christ. And as this generation catches hold of that truth, we will see a shift in the spiritual atmosphere like never before.

Identity is the foundation of everything. When you know who you are in Christ, it impacts how you live, how you love, and how you fulfill your purpose.

The Identity Revolution is not just about self-discovery; it's about God-discovery. It's about young adults awakening to the truth that their value, purpose, and destiny are found in Christ alone. When you know who you are, you can stand firm against the lies of the enemy.

This revolution will lead to a generation that no longer seeks approval from the world but walks confidently in their God-given calling. They will no longer conform to the patterns of this world, but they will be transformed by the renewing of their minds (Romans 12:2). This transformation will birth a movement of radical discipleship, purpose-driven living, and Kingdom impact.

A Prophetic Call: The Time is Now

As I speak these words, I sense the urgency of the moment. The time is now for an Identity Revolution. The same God who brought revival through the Jesus Movement, who restored truth through the Reformation, is preparing to unleash a new wave of transformation in our day. This is not a revolution of man—it's a move of God.

And it starts with you. You are part of this Identity Revolution. As you go through this book and 21-Day Devotion, God will awaken your heart to the truth of who you are in Him. You will begin to see yourself as God sees you, and you will step into the fullness of the identity He has given you. This is your moment to break free from the lies, from the confusion, from the chains that have held you back. This is your moment to join the Identity Revolution.

As we begin this journey, I invite you to open your heart, your mind, and your spirit to the transforming truth of God's Word. This is more than a devotional—it's a revolution. A revolution that will change

Discover Who You Are

how you see yourself, how you live, and how you impact the world around you.

The Identity Revolution is here. The only question is, will you be part of it?

Chapter 1
The War for Your Identity

In a world obsessed with image, influence, and *'finding yourself,'* one truth stands out: knowing who you are—and more importantly, whose you are—is foundational. You can change careers, reinvent yourself, or chase the latest trends, but there's only one identity that truly anchors you, and that's the identity given by Christ. The reality is that the battle for your life begins with the battle for your identity.

Think about it. When you know who you are in Christ, you live with confidence, purpose, and clarity. But when you're unsure, life becomes a constant game of catch-up, trying to fit into whatever mold the world tosses your way. The world will tell you to be one thing today, and something else tomorrow, always keeping you guessing.

> If you don't know who you are, you'll always be at the mercy of who the world says you should be.

This isn't just a cultural issue; it's spiritual warfare. At the core of every attack, every whisper of doubt, is a strategy to distort your understanding of who God made you to be. Consider this: before we even come to terms with what God says about us, the enemy is already hard at work, trying to implant lies. These lies often sound harmless at first—questions about your worth, comparisons that eat away at your confidence, or temptations to measure your value by what you achieve. But over time, they accumulate, leading you away from the truth.

It's no coincidence that identity is the first thing under attack in nearly every spiritual battle. Whether it's through the voices of culture, past mistakes, or unmet expectations, the enemy knows that confusion in your identity creates chaos in your life. Why? Because when you're unclear about who you are, you're also unclear about whose you are. And when that happens, your purpose and direction can feel like shifting sand.

But here's the truth: God didn't create us to live in uncertainty. From the moment He breathed life into us, He called us by name, marked us with His image, and set us apart for His purpose. This isn't just a nice thought; it's a profound reality. Your identity in Christ is secure, unchanging, and powerful—and when you embrace it, it shapes every part of your life.

As we move forward, we'll uncover how to recognize the enemy's lies and replace them with God's truth. This journey isn't just about defending who you are—it's about reclaiming who God says you've always been.

The Enemy's Agenda – Identity Theft

The enemy has a singular, unrelenting mission when it comes to your identity: to disconnect you from the truth of who God says you are. He knows that when you're confident in your identity, you walk in purpose, freedom, and strength. But if he can shake that confidence—just a little—he can influence everything from your decisions to your sense of worth. This isn't a new tactic. From the very beginning, Satan's strategy has revolved around one thing: identity theft.

Consider the first recorded conversation between Satan and humanity, with Eve in the Garden of Eden. Satan doesn't launch an outright attack; he plants a question, a subtle doubt: *"Did God really say...?"* In that moment, he isn't just questioning God's words—he's undermining Eve's understanding of her place with God. The goal? To get her to question, even for a second, her identity as one who is loved, protected, and created by God. When doubt enters the picture, security leaves.

What Satan knows is that when you're unsure of who you are, it's easy to believe lies about what you're supposed to be. Eve's identity was rooted in being made in God's image, but Satan's whisper of doubt started to chip away at that foundation. And from that small question, everything unraveled. The enemy doesn't need a full-on assault; he only needs a crack to weaken the foundation.

Fast forward to the wilderness, where Satan encounters Jesus. Here, Satan uses the same approach, beginning with, *"If you are the Son of God…"* Notice the word if. He's trying to plant a seed of doubt in Jesus' identity. Satan knew Jesus was the Son of God, but he also knew that an ounce of doubt can cause a mountain of hesitation. If Satan could shake even Jesus' confidence, he thought he might derail His mission.

But Jesus doesn't entertain the enemy's taunts. He answers not from a place of insecurity, but with the unshakable confidence of knowing exactly who He is. Jesus' response to the enemy is rooted in His identity as God's Son, and that confidence leaves no room for the enemy to gain ground.

The enemy uses these same tactics on us today, trying to pry us away from the truth of our identity. He whispers doubts, magnifies insecurities, and throws up smoke screens of comparison—all designed to make us feel *"less than"* or *"not enough."* And if we're not careful, these whispers can lead us to question our worth, our purpose, and our standing with God.

But here's the truth that we need to cling to:

> **When our identity is grounded in Christ, the enemy's lies lose their power.**

When we know who we are in God, no amount of doubt or deception can shake us. Satan's agenda may be identity theft, but God's agenda is to secure our identity in Him—a foundation that can't be stolen, corrupted, or changed.

The Power of Imago Dei (Image of God)

At the core of our identity lies a powerful truth: we are made in the Image of God. This isn't just a theological statement; it's the foundation of who we are. The Latin term Imago Dei, meaning *"Image of God,"* speaks to the essence of our creation. God didn't make us by accident or mold us from some template; He created each of us intentionally, reflecting aspects of His character, His love, and His creativity in us. Imago Dei means we were handcrafted by God, and that's a reality that changes everything.

Being made in God's image means we're more than just physical beings; we're a reflection of the Creator Himself. God chose to give us the unique capacity to love, to create, to reason, and to connect with Him in a way that nothing else in creation can. This truth forms the bedrock of our identity and our worth. If we're reflections of God, then every part of us carries purpose and value that the world could never define or diminish.

This is why Imago Dei is such a powerful concept. When we understand we're created in God's image, we don't just find value in ourselves; we find value that is rooted in the unchanging character of God. No trend, no failure, and no opinion can alter that.

In a world where worth is often defined by achievement, appearance, or approval, Imago Dei offers a radical counterpoint. Your value doesn't fluctuate with your success or your social standing—it's anchored in the fact that you're a reflection of the Creator. The truth of Imago Dei shatters every lie that tells you you're not enough, that you're insignificant, or that you have to strive to be valued.

Think about that. The world says, *"Prove your worth."* God says, *"Your worth is already established in Me."* Our identity isn't something we earn; it's something we're given. Knowing you're made in God's image brings a confidence and a freedom that can't be shaken. It means you don't have to hustle for approval or seek validation from temporary sources. You can rest in the reality that you are already loved, known, and valued by the One who designed you.

When we embrace the truth of Imago Dei, it changes how we see ourselves—and it changes how we live. We begin to realize that we carry God's image in every interaction, every decision, and every relationship. Our actions reflect our Creator, and our lives point back to Him. This isn't about perfection; it's about purpose.

> Living out Imago Dei means understanding that our identity is a divine reflection, a daily reminder that we are God's masterpiece.

Each day, we have a choice: to live out the image of God within us or to let the world define who we should be. Embracing Imago Dei isn't just acknowledging a theological truth; it's reclaiming the identity that God placed within us from the very beginning. And when we walk in that identity, we don't just live differently—we live in the fullness of who God created us to be.

Recognizing the Counterfeits

When we begin to understand that we're created in God's image, something shifts. But even as we start to grasp this truth, the enemy works overtime to push counterfeit identities into our lives—cheap substitutes that undermine our God-given worth. He uses subtle lies to distort our sense of self, hoping we'll exchange the truth of Imago Dei for hollow, temporary labels. Let's confront three of these common lies with a clear understanding of how they seek to rob us of our true identity.

Lie #1: You Are Only as Good as What You Achieve

One of the enemy's favorite lies is that our worth is directly tied to our accomplishments. This lie tells us that we're valuable only if we're successful, productive, and impressive. It tempts us to believe that our identity is a never-ending checklist, and as long as we're checking off achievements, we're worth something. But the moment we fail or don't measure up, our value plummets. This is the cycle of performance-driven worth: always striving, never secure.

God's Truth: The Bible is clear—our worth isn't tied to our productivity or achievements. In Ephesians 2:8-9, Paul reminds us that we are saved by grace, not by our works. If God's love isn't

> Our identity is secure, not because of what we accomplish, but because of what God has already accomplished in us.

dependent on what we achieve, then our identity isn't either. We are loved because we belong to Him, not because we've earned it.

Lie #2: If People Don't Approve of You, You're Failing

Another subtle but powerful lie is the need for approval. This lie tells us that if we don't have others' validation, we're somehow falling short. It tricks us into believing that our identity is up for debate, depending on who we're around and how much they approve. We start to live our lives in ways that earn the praise of others, even if it means sacrificing parts of who we truly are. Approval becomes a trap, and we become people-pleasers instead of God-pleasers.

God's Truth: Galatians 1:10 calls us to live for God, not for human approval: *"If I were still trying to please people, I would not be a servant of Christ."* Our identity in Christ frees us from the pressure to perform for others.

> When we know we are approved by God, the opinions of others lose

This truth breaks the chains of people-pleasing and grounds us in a confidence that can't be swayed by public opinion.

Lie #3: You'll Never Be Enough

Perhaps the most damaging lie of all is the belief that we're inherently lacking, that no matter how hard we try, we'll never measure up. This lie tells us that we're flawed at the core, that our weaknesses make us unworthy, and that we'll never truly be enough for God or anyone else. It's a lie that leads to shame, insecurity, and hopelessness. It keeps us focused on our limitations, convincing us that our flaws define us.

God's Truth: In 2 Corinthians 12:9, God's response to our weakness is grace: *"My grace is sufficient for you, for my power is made perfect in weakness."* God doesn't see our weaknesses as limitations; He sees them as opportunities to show His strength through us.

> Our value isn't based on being "enough" in the world's eyes—it's found in being loved and chosen by God, just as we are.

This truth reminds us that we are complete in Christ, not because we're perfect, but because His love fills every gap.

These lies—achievement-based worth, approval-seeking, and the feeling of never being enough—are the enemy's counterfeit attempts to keep us from living in the truth of who God says we are. Recognizing these lies is the first step to reclaiming our true identity. With every truth we cling to, we dismantle the enemy's counterfeits and take one step closer to embracing the fullness of Imago Dei in our lives.

Reclaiming the Truth

Recognizing the lies is only half the battle; the real power comes when we actively reclaim the truth of who God says we are. Every day, we're faced with a choice: to live according to the world's fleeting definitions or to stand firm in the eternal identity God has given us.

> Reclaiming our identity in Christ isn't a one-time realization—it's a daily decision.

Here are three practical steps to anchor ourselves in God's truth and silence the lies.

Step 1: Identify the Lie

The first step in reclaiming truth is becoming aware of the lies that slip into our minds. These lies often sound familiar and may even echo past experiences or insecurities, making them seem convincing. But when a thought contradicts what God says about us, we need to call it out for what it is—a distortion of the truth.

A helpful question to ask ourselves is, *"Does this thought align with God's Word?"* If it doesn't, we know it's not from God. The enemy's lies can be subtle, but God's truth is clear. Identifying the lies brings them out of the shadows and into the light, where we can confront them with truth.

Step 2: Replace with Truth

Once we identify the lie, we have to replace it with God's truth. Simply recognizing a lie isn't enough; we need to actively fill that space with words of life from Scripture. This is where God's promises become our weapon. For every lie, there's a truth in God's Word that counters it. If we're tempted to believe we're only as valuable as our achievements, we can lean into Ephesians 2:10, where God declares that we are His masterpiece, created with purpose. If we're feeling *"not enough,"* we can remember 2 Corinthians 12:9, where God's power shines through our weaknesses.

This isn't about positive thinking; it's about truth-filled thinking. The goal is to replace the enemy's lies with Scripture so that God's voice becomes the loudest in our minds. With each truth we hold onto, we push back against the enemy's attempts to distort our identity.

Step 3: Walk in Faith

Reclaiming our identity also means walking in faith, even when it's difficult to believe the truth. There will be days when the lies feel louder than the truth, but that's when faith steps in. Faith isn't about ignoring doubts; it's about choosing to trust God's Word above everything else. When we walk in faith, we're not just acknowledging God's truth; we're living it out.

Walking in faith transforms our identity from an idea we believe to a reality we experience. It means we choose to act on what God says about us, even when we feel otherwise. This might look like speaking truth over ourselves when we're discouraged or reminding ourselves of God's promises when insecurities rise up. Each step of faith strengthens our confidence and keeps us grounded in who God says we are.

These three steps—identifying the lie, replacing it with truth, and walking in faith—are practical ways to reclaim our God-given identity. Each time we put these steps into practice, we're reinforcing our true identity and silencing the voices that try to pull us away from it. Reclaiming the truth is a journey, but it's a journey toward freedom, security, and purpose. As we choose to live in God's truth, the enemy's lies lose their power, and we step into the fullness of who we were created to be.

Seeing Yourself Through God's Eyes

The way we see ourselves shapes how we live. If we only see ourselves through the lens of our flaws, mistakes, or the world's ever-shifting standards, we end up with a distorted view of who we truly are. But what if we could see ourselves the way God sees us? God's perspective isn't clouded by insecurities, failures, or societal expectations. When He looks at us, He sees His beloved creation—a reflection of His love, purpose, and grace.

Imagine how different life would be if you fully embraced God's view of you. He sees you as His child, created in His image, uniquely designed and equipped with purpose. In Isaiah 43:1, God says, *"Do not fear, for I have redeemed you; I have called you by name; you are mine."* These words are more than comforting—they're transformational. To be seen through God's eyes is to be known fully and loved completely. There's no striving, no need for approval, and no fear of rejection in His gaze.

When we take on God's perspective, we begin to let go of the false identities we've held onto. We realize we're not defined by our failures or limited by our weaknesses. Instead, we're defined by the One who calls us His own, who sees our potential, and who loves us unconditionally.

Seeing ourselves through God's eyes isn't just about feeling good; it's about transformation. When we embrace how God sees us, it influences every part of our lives. It changes how we interact with others, how we respond to challenges, and how we approach our purpose. Living out of our true identity in Christ means living with confidence, purpose, and joy—not because of who we are on our own, but because of who we are in Him.

When we see ourselves as God's beloved children, we stop striving for acceptance and start living from a place of acceptance. This shift frees us from the need to constantly prove ourselves, allowing us to rest in the assurance that we are already enough in His eyes. And in that place of security, we can love others more freely, serve more selflessly, and step into our purpose with greater boldness.

In a world where people often feel the need to hide their true selves, God invites us into a freedom that can only be found in being fully known and fully loved.

> **There's no part of you that God doesn't see, and there's no part of you that He doesn't love.**

This reality is what allows us to shed the false identities and embrace who we are in Him. We're free to be our true selves—unapologetically, authentically, and fully—as we walk in His love.

Seeing yourself through God's eyes is more than a perspective shift; it's a transformative experience that grounds your identity in something eternal, unshakable, and deeply personal. When you align your vision with His, you'll find freedom, security, and purpose that nothing in the world can offer. And in that place of divine perspective, you'll be empowered to live as the person He created you to be—a reflection of His image, a bearer of His love, and a child of His heart.

Chapter 2
Mirrors and Masks – The Image We Reflect

We all have moments when we look in the mirror and ask ourselves, *"Who am I, really?"* This question cuts deeper than what we see on the surface. The mirror can reflect our physical features, sure, but it rarely shows what's happening beneath—our true identity, buried under layers of roles, expectations, and insecurities.

> Mirrors might reveal our face, but only God's view reveals our identity.

This question of *"who we are"* is critical because how we see ourselves shapes everything we do. Our approach to relationships, challenges, and even our purpose flows from our perception of our identity. Yet, if we're honest, many of us aren't entirely sure who we truly are. We know our titles, our accomplishments, and the roles we play, but knowing our true identity requires us to go beyond the mirror and look through the lens of God's perspective.

Discover Who You Are

Think of all the different *"yours"* that you bring into various spaces. There's the *"you"* at work, the *"you"* with friends, the *"you"* at home. And while each of these versions may be a genuine part of who you are, they're just fragments. At the core, there's a single identity that transcends these roles. But if we spend too much time looking into the world's mirrors—mirrors that reflect only what society expects us to be—we can lose sight of that core identity. We're not defined by the fragments others see but by the whole person God created us to be.

Here's the tricky part: self-reflection, the world tells us, is the key to finding ourselves. But if all we're doing is reflecting on who we think we should be, or worse, on who others think we should be, we're not likely to find our true selves.

> **The more we stare into the mirror of our own expectations or society's standards, the more distorted our self-image becomes.**

Instead of truly seeing ourselves, we start to see only the *"should"* and the *"supposed-to's."* "*I should be more successful.*" "I'm supposed to be perfect." "*I should have it all together by now.*" But God invites us to look past the *"shoulds"* and see the person He made us to be—loved, chosen, and purposeful.

Identity Revolution

The world's mirror and God's mirror reflect two very different images. The world's mirror shows us a reflection based on appearance, status, and achievements. It's a mirror that's constantly shifting, distorting who we are with each new trend or expectation. In the world's mirror, our worth is always up for debate, dependent on the latest opinions or comparisons.

But God's mirror is different. God's mirror reflects back an unchanging image, one that doesn't depend on our achievements, our looks, or anyone else's approval. When God looks at us, He doesn't see a collection of roles or accomplishments; He sees His masterpiece. When God is your mirror, you see the masterpiece He created—not the flawed image the world wants you to believe.

The Masks We Wear – Why We Hide

We all wear masks from time to time, don't we? Whether it's the *"I've got it all together"* mask we bring to work or the *"nothing bothers me"* mask we wear around friends, these fronts often serve as shields against vulnerability.

> **Masks can feel safe, but they also keep us hidden from the very connection we crave.**

The reality is, we wear masks for different reasons. Sometimes we're afraid of being judged, so we put on a *"perfect"* front. Other times, we worry that our real selves won't be accepted, so we put on a mask that we think others will like.

When we try too hard to fit into roles or expectations, we end up disconnected from our true selves—and ultimately from God, who sees through our masks.

> **A mask might win you applause, but only authenticity brings peace.**

Masks often start as defense mechanisms, something we put on in moments of insecurity. Maybe we didn't feel *"enough"* in some area, so we put on a mask to cover up what we think are our shortcomings. The problem is, these masks can quickly become a lifestyle. They keep us locked into a version of ourselves that's based on fear rather than truth.

> **When we rely on masks, we're choosing the safety of acceptance over the freedom of authenticity.**

Consider the *"Put-Together Professional,"* who's constantly working to maintain an image of success, or the *"People-Pleaser,"* who tries to be everything to everyone just to avoid conflict. While these personas might bring temporary validation, they also bring an endless need for approval. Each mask we wear distances us from the authentic person God created us to be.

Over time, masks don't just hide us; they start to define us. When we wear them for too long, it becomes hard to remember who we are beneath them. And as we focus on keeping up appearances, we begin to lose sight of the identity God designed for us. Living behind a mask might protect us from rejection, but it also keeps us from truly living.

God calls us to authenticity, not as a burden, but as an invitation. In Him, we're free to lay down our masks, to be known and loved exactly as we are. When we drop the facade, we step into a place of true freedom, one where we don't have to impress or perform. We simply have to show up as the person God created us to be.

Mirrors are supposed to show us who we are, but they're not always honest, are they? Beyond the literal mirror, we have "mirrors" all around us—the reflections of ourselves that we see in social media, in the opinions of others, or in the achievements of our peers. But these mirrors rarely tell the full truth. Comparison is a mirror that distorts the image of who you really are.

When we start comparing ourselves to others, it's like looking into a carnival mirror that warps reality. We see people's polished, filtered highlights and feel like we're falling short. We see what others have achieved and start measuring our own worth against it. This kind of comparison-driven reflection creates a distorted self-image, leaving us feeling like we're *"less than"* or *"not enough."* The world's mirrors twist our perspective, convincing us that we'll never measure up to an illusion.

The more we look to external mirrors to define our worth, the more we rely on shifting, unstable standards. We begin to judge ourselves by what we lack rather than what we have, by what we think we should be rather than who we are. And the more we look at others, the less we see ourselves through the lens of God's truth. When we let culture define us, we end up reflecting the world instead of the image of God.

This constant comparison and striving for validation can easily lead us into a cycle of dissatisfaction. We chase approval, likes, and recognition, thinking they will satisfy us, but they're a moving target. There's always another achievement, another milestone, another person who seems to have what we don't. Looking at ourselves through the lens of comparison only leaves us feeling hollow and disconnected from who God says we are.

God's Word: The True Mirror

In James 1:23-24, we're reminded that God's Word is the ultimate mirror. It reflects back not only who we are but who we're becoming in Him. Unlike the world's mirrors, which highlight our flaws or show us an incomplete picture, God's mirror shows us our true identity as His beloved creation. When we look into the mirror of God's Word, we find a reflection that isn't distorted but beautifully honest.

God's mirror invites us to stop comparing and start seeing ourselves as He sees us—whole, valued, and loved. It breaks the cycle of comparison because it's grounded in a truth that doesn't change. When we focus on His reflection, we let go of the distorted views that tell us we're not enough and embrace the unchanging truth that we are already more than enough in Him.

If we want to understand our true identity, we have to choose the right mirror. God's Word is the only mirror that reflects back who we are in a way that doesn't change with trends, opinions, or achievements. When we look into this true mirror, we see ourselves not through the lens of our flaws or limitations but as God sees us—His beloved creation, made in His image. When God is your mirror, you see the masterpiece He created, not the flawed image the world wants you to believe.

Looking into God's mirror is about more than self-acceptance; it's about transformation. As we take in His perspective, we start to see that our identity isn't something we create or earn—it's something He's given. We are His children, made with purpose, loved without condition, and called to reflect His character. God's mirror doesn't distort; it clarifies and affirms who we are in Him.

In 2 Corinthians 3:18, Paul describes how we're transformed into the image of Christ as we behold His glory. This isn't a superficial change but a deep transformation that shapes how we see ourselves and how we live. When we allow God's Word to be our mirror, we're reminded of the incredible reality that we're not defined by our failures, our insecurities, or the world's opinions, but by God's unchanging truth.

Reflecting God's image means embracing who He's called us to be, unapologetically. We don't have to hide parts of ourselves or wear masks to be accepted. Living out of our true identity in Christ means living with confidence, not because of who we are on our own, but because of who we are in Him. There's a freedom that comes with this truth. When we stop looking to the world's mirrors and start embracing the reflection of God's mirror, we walk with a sense of purpose and assurance that nothing else can provide.

To reflect God's image isn't just about seeing ourselves differently; it's about showing others who He is through our lives. Every day, we have an opportunity to live in a way that reflects His love, grace, and truth to those around us. Living out Imago Dei means understanding that our identity is a divine reflection, a daily reminder that we are God's masterpiece. This changes not just how

Identity Revolution

we see ourselves but how we interact with the world, bringing God's light into every space we enter.

When we embrace the true mirror of God's Word, we're no longer trapped by the need for approval or validation. Instead, we live as the people God created us to be, reflecting His image confidently and freely. This is the power of seeing ourselves as God sees us—a power that frees us to be our authentic, redeemed, and beloved selves.

Breaking Free from the Masks

To live in the fullness of who God created us to be, we must shed the masks that keep us hidden. While masks can feel like a shield, they also weigh us down, preventing us from stepping into the freedom and authenticity God desires for us.

> Freedom begins when we take off the mask and let God's truth shape our identity.

Step 1: Recognize Your Masks

The first step in breaking free is acknowledging the masks we wear. Often, these masks become so much a part of us that we forget we're even wearing them. Maybe we put on a mask of *"strength"* to avoid showing weakness, or we adopt a mask of *"success"* to feel valued.

These masks might bring temporary acceptance, but they also keep us from experiencing the joy of being truly known.

To live authentically in Christ, we have to get honest about where we're hiding. This isn't about shame; it's about freedom. When we bring our masks into the light, they lose their power over us. God invites us to come as we are, without pretense, because He sees through every mask and loves us completely.

Step 2: Lay Down the Masks

Once we've identified our masks, we need to intentionally lay them down. This doesn't mean we suddenly stop caring about others' opinions or become immune to insecurities. But it does mean we choose to prioritize God's view over the world's. Laying down our masks might look like letting go of the need to be *"perfect,"* saying no to things that don't align with our values, or speaking honestly even when it's uncomfortable. Letting go of our masks is a choice to live from a place of authenticity, trusting that who we are in Christ is enough.

This step may require prayer, support, and even some vulnerability, but each time we let go of a mask, we're choosing the freedom of living as God's true reflection. God's love fills the spaces we once felt needed to be hidden.

Step 3: Walk in the Image of God

Finally, living authentically means embracing our identity as image-bearers of Christ. This isn't just about not hiding; it's about reflecting His character in everything we do. We no longer need to strive for approval or seek validation from shifting sources. When we walk in the image of God, we're secure in the truth that we are chosen, valued, and loved beyond measure.

Walking in the image of God gives us confidence to show up as we are—flaws and all—because we know we're not defined by them.

> **True authenticity isn't found in being perfect; it's found in being real.**

Instead, we're defined by the One who created us with purpose and love. And in God's eyes, being real is enough.

Living Authentically: A Daily Journey

Breaking free from our masks and living authentically in Christ is a journey, not a destination. It's a daily choice to see ourselves through God's eyes, to live as His reflection, and to embrace our identity without apology. As we make this choice each day, we'll find a freedom and joy that no mask could ever offer. In Christ, we don't have to hide; we get to live fully, boldly, and authentically, just as He created us to be.

When we embrace our true identity in Christ, we discover a confidence that no mask or role could ever provide. This confidence isn't about arrogance or self-reliance; it's rooted in the assurance of who we are in Him. When you know who you are in Christ, you can live with a boldness that doesn't waver with opinions or trends. This is the freedom God invites us into—a life where we reflect His image unapologetically, with grace and humility.

The world often tells us to be "*confident*," but it bases confidence on what we do or what we have. God, however, calls us to a different kind of confidence—one that rests not in ourselves but in who He is.

> Our confidence isn't built on shifting accomplishments or approval; it's anchored in the unchanging love of God.

This means that even when we face criticism, failure, or insecurity, our sense of self doesn't falter, because it's built on a foundation that cannot be moved.

When we live from this place of God-given confidence, we're no longer afraid to show up as we truly are. We don't need to downplay our strengths or hide our weaknesses. Instead, we can live openly, letting others see Christ in us, flaws and all. Confidence in Christ gives us the courage to be seen and to let God's light shine through every part of who we are.

Living with confidence in our true identity doesn't mean we'll get it right every time. We'll still have moments of doubt or times when we slip back into old habits of comparison or mask-wearing. But the beauty of our identity in Christ is that it isn't based on perfection; it's based on His grace. True confidence is knowing we don't have to be perfect to reflect Christ—we simply need to be willing.

In 1 Peter 2:9, we're called a *"chosen people, a royal priesthood, a holy nation, God's special possession."* This is our identity, one that we can embrace without fear or apology. We don't have to fit into the world's molds or prove our worth because God has already claimed us as His own. Reflecting Christ without apology means embracing this identity wholeheartedly, letting it shape our lives, and not shrinking back because of what others might think.

When we walk confidently in our identity, we inspire others to do the same. People are drawn to authenticity, and when we live in alignment with who God created us to be, we invite others to experience that same freedom. Reflecting Christ without apology is an act of love, not only to ourselves but to those around us. It shows the world that true confidence isn't about putting on a facade but about living in the fullness of God's truth.

As we journey forward, let's remember that this confidence isn't something we muster up; it's a gift God gives to those who walk in His light. We don't have to hide or hold back. In Christ, we're free to be bold, to be real, and to be exactly who He created us to be.

Chapter 3
Gender and the Gift of Identity

In today's world, identity—especially gender identity—has become one of the most complex and talked-about topics. Everywhere we look, society is presenting new ideas about what it means to *"find ourselves." The old question of "Who am I?"* has taken on a new dimension, often turning into, *"What do I feel?"* It's become common for people to question everything about themselves based on shifting emotions or cultural pressures. And while asking questions can be healthy, we've reached a point where clarity has been traded for confusion.

It's almost humorous when you think about it—there was a time when the hardest part of introducing ourselves was just saying our name. Now, there's an entire spectrum of labels and pronouns to consider. Even the most basic interactions come with an added layer of complexity. Who knew that introducing yourself could become a vocabulary lesson?

But here's the thing: identity isn't just what we feel; it's who we're made to be. While emotions are real and can shape how we experience the world, they're not designed to be the foundation of who we are. Feelings shift with circumstances, but truth remains steady. Imagine building a house on sand versus on a rock—one will constantly shift and need adjustment, while the other stands firm no matter the storm.

The idea that identity can be as fluid as our feelings is appealing because it gives us control. But just because something feels right in the moment doesn't mean it aligns with the truth of who we are. Our identity, especially our gender, is more than a journey of self-discovery; it's a gift of God's design.

As we dive into this chapter, we'll look at the foundational truths that ground our identity—biological, scientific, and, ultimately, spiritual. Because the journey to understanding ourselves isn't just about looking inward; it's about looking up, seeing who God made us to be, and letting His design shape our self-understanding.

The Biology Behind Identity

At the core of our physical identity, there's a reality that no amount of shifting trends or changing opinions can alter: our biology. While society might debate what it means to be male or female, biology itself speaks with clarity.

> **Our DNA is God's blueprint for our bodies, reminding us that our design is intentional, not incidental.**

Science and faith might seem like separate worlds, but when it comes to identity, they actually confirm each other in powerful ways.

From the very beginning of life, biology determines whether we are male or female. Every cell in our body contains a genetic code, and this code isn't random or vague—it's precise. We inherit 23 chromosomes from each parent, and one of these pairs is our sex chromosomes: XX for females and XY for males. This chromosomal blueprint sets the stage for our biological sex, guiding the development of our bodies in specific ways. Our DNA doesn't just describe who we are; it declares it with certainty.

This isn't simply a matter of physical features or external appearances. Our sex chromosomes influence a range of biological processes; from the way our brains develop to how our hormones function. These biological distinctions are not trivial—they're essential, forming the basis of who we are as individuals. It's as if our bodies are constantly echoing God's design, saying, *"You were made with purpose."*

Beyond chromosomes, there's another powerful biological component that reinforces our identity: hormones. Males and females have different hormonal balances, primarily testosterone in males and estrogen in females. These hormones shape our bodies in unique ways, influencing everything from muscle mass to reproductive function. It's not just about what we see on the outside; these hormones impact how we process experiences, how we relate to others, and even how we think.

Imagine if we tried to tell our hormones to behave differently based on how we felt one day. It would be a bit like arguing with gravity—it simply doesn't work. Turns out, testosterone and estrogen don't ask for our opinions; they have their own ideas about who we are. These biological markers serve as a reminder that our identity is more deeply rooted than shifting emotions or societal labels. They anchor us to a reality that's hard-wired into our very being.

It's easy to assume that science and faith are at odds, but the truth is, they often tell the same story in different ways. While science can show us how our bodies work, faith reveals why they were made that way.

> Science can show us how we're made, but only faith can show us why we're made.

The biological reality of male and female isn't just a scientific fact—it's a reflection of God's intentionality. Genesis 1:27 tells us that God created us in His image, *"male and female He created them."* This wasn't an arbitrary choice; it was a deliberate act, embedding purpose into our very structure. When we embrace the truth of our biology, we're not rejecting progress or ignoring feelings—we're aligning ourselves with the design that God has built into the world.

Our bodies, our DNA, our chromosomes—they aren't barriers to self-expression; they're evidence of divine craftsmanship. In a world that's constantly telling us to redefine ourselves, biology offers a steady reminder that some things are simply true. And it's in this truth, unchanging and beautifully crafted, that we find a firm foundation for our identity.

The Biblical Perspective on Gender

While science provides us with the *"how"* of our identity, the Bible offers us the *"why."* In a world where definitions and labels are constantly shifting, Scripture stands as a solid foundation, reminding us that gender is not just a physical trait but a profound part of God's design. *"We're not just bodies with parts; we're reflections of God's heart."* Our gender isn't something we decide; it's something God has lovingly crafted into us, expressing His image in a way that's both intentional and beautiful.

Discover Who You Are

In the opening chapters of Genesis, we see God's plan for humanity unfold with deliberate care. Genesis 1:27 declares, *"So God created mankind in His own image, in the image of God He created them; male and female He created them."* Notice the repetition here—it's as though Scripture is emphasizing that our creation as male and female is central to God's design. God didn't make us one way by accident and another by preference; He made us male and female on purpose.

This distinction isn't just about anatomy or function; it's about identity. Male and female reflect different aspects of God's nature. Together, they reveal a fuller picture of His character, His creativity, and His relational nature. Just as God is three-in-one—Father, Son, and Holy Spirit—humanity, created as male and female, reflects a unity in diversity.

> **Gender isn't an accident or an add-on; it's part of the profound way we bear God's image.**

God's intentional design in creating male and female was to bring balance, not division. Gender is not a hierarchy but a complementarity—a way for each of us to bring unique strengths to the table. We see this dynamic in marriage, where men and women are called to serve, honor, and love one another as equals, yet with roles that reflect their distinct gifts. Ephesians 5:22-33, for example, describes the mutual submission and love within marriage, a partnership where both male and female are needed to reflect the love of Christ and His church.

When we understand gender as a gift, we begin to see that it is not a restriction or limitation but an invitation to live fully within God's design. In God's design, male and female aren't labels to divide us; they're gifts that connect us. Each gender brings something valuable to relationships, families, and communities. And when we embrace our roles without envy or competition, we honor the way God has wired us to live and relate.

Throughout the Bible, we see countless examples of men and women fulfilling unique purposes. Deborah, a judge and leader, exemplifies courage and wisdom (Judges 4-5), while David's life reflects the strength and humility of a man after God's heart (1 Samuel 13:14). Jesus Himself demonstrated profound respect and value for women, breaking cultural norms to reveal their dignity and worth, as with the Samaritan woman at the well (John 4) and Mary Magdalene, whom He entrusted with the news of His resurrection (John 20:16-18).

In these examples, gender isn't diminished or blurred—it's celebrated. Men and women, each with their unique roles, participate in God's redemptive story, revealing His heart to the world. God's design brings balance and harmony, inviting us to live out our purpose without erasing the distinctions He has given us.

When we see gender from a biblical perspective, we realize that male and female are not just biological realities or social constructs—they're a reflection of God Himself. To live out our identity as men and women is to participate in something sacred. God calls us to honor the gifts and distinctions He has given, not to blur or erase them in the name of convenience or cultural trends.

> **The beauty of God's design is that our identity is already complete in Him, created with intention and love.**

Embracing our gender as part of God's plan allows us to live confidently, knowing that our identity is not something we need to redefine but something we are invited to live out. Gender is a divine gift, a way for us to reflect His glory uniquely, together.

The Cultural Confusion

In today's culture, the conversation around gender has become increasingly complex, often detached from biological or biblical truth. Society is now filled with voices claiming that gender is fluid, self-determined, or simply a social construct. While these ideas are presented as progressive, they introduce confusion rather than clarity. The Bible and science both offer us a consistent, reliable foundation for understanding identity.

> **Feelings are real, but they don't rewrite biology.**

Let's address some of the myths that are frequently promoted and examine how they measure up to truth.

Myth #1: Gender is Just a Social Construct

This myth claims that gender is an arbitrary label created by society. According to this view, people should be free to choose or change their gender based on personal preference, as gender supposedly has no grounding in physical reality. While society does influence certain behaviors associated with gender roles (such as boys liking blue and girls liking pink), these cultural preferences are not the same as biological identity.

The Truth: Gender isn't a construct; it's a cornerstone. Studies in neuroscience and psychology have consistently shown that men and women have unique physiological and psychological traits, shaped by biological differences. For example, differences in brain structure and hormonal influence between males and females lead to distinct ways of processing emotions, problem-solving, and even social

Discover Who You Are

interaction. Our biology doesn't just inform our bodies—it shapes our perspectives, preferences, and strengths.

By dismissing gender as a social construct, we ignore the depth and complexity of God's design.

> Gender isn't a costume to put on; it's an intrinsic part of who we are, woven into our

Myth #2: You Can Change Your Gender to Match How You Feel

This myth suggests that if someone feels like they belong to a different gender, they should alter their bodies to match that feeling. From hormones to surgeries, people are told that changing their appearance will align their internal feelings with their external reality. While it's true that some people experience deep discomfort with their biological sex (known as gender dysphoria), science shows us that changing one's body does not necessarily resolve this discomfort. In fact, studies have shown that even after transitioning, rates of anxiety, depression, and suicidal ideation remain high among those who struggle with gender dysphoria.

The Truth: Feelings can be incredibly powerful, but they don't override biological facts. Research shows that when people are treated with compassion and given counseling to understand their feelings rather than alter their bodies, many experience peace with their biological identity. Our bodies are not problems to be fixed; they are a gift to be understood and valued.

As believers, we acknowledge that God created us intentionally and with purpose. While struggles with identity are real and should be met with compassion, the answer isn't found in altering our God-given bodies.

> True peace isn't found in changing our bodies; it's found in understanding our worth.

Myth #3: Gender Fluidity Means We're Evolving Beyond the Binary

A popular claim today is that embracing a range of gender identities is a sign of societal evolution. This myth suggests that being "*gender fluid*" or non-binary is a progressive step toward inclusivity. However, when we look at biology and psychology, we find that humans have consistently demonstrated a binary understanding of gender across cultures and centuries.

The Truth: Science confirms the biological binary of male and female. Every human cell, from skin cells to neurons, carries chromosomes that mark us as male or female. While there are rare intersex conditions, these do not represent a third gender but rather a medical anomaly affecting physical development. Evolutionary biology shows us that the binary is essential for reproduction and survival. The binary of male and female isn't limiting; it's life-giving.

Even historically, societies have recognized this binary framework, honoring the unique roles and contributions of men and women. Moving away from this binary isn't evolution; it's a departure from the foundational design that God established. In honoring the binary, we reflect God's intentionality and design for human life.

Myth #4: Accepting All Gender Identities is a Way to Show Love

This myth promotes the idea that to love others, we must affirm every expression of identity, including non-biblical views of gender. Love, according to this perspective, is equated with total acceptance and endorsement, without questioning or challenging. But biblically, love goes deeper than simple affirmation. True love is compassionate and courageous, willing to speak truth even when it's uncomfortable.

The Truth: Love doesn't mean agreeing with everything someone believes about themselves. In 1 Corinthians 13, we're reminded that love *"rejoices with the truth."* Jesus showed us that love can be compassionate and corrective at the same time—He met people where they were but didn't leave them there.

> True love is willing to say the hard thing when it leads to healing.

As believers, we are called to speak truth in love, guiding people toward an understanding of God's design for them. To love others well, we don't ignore what Scripture and science reveal about identity. Instead, we offer a perspective that aligns with both truth and compassion.

Myth #5: If It Feels Right, It Must Be True

This final myth reflects a deeper trend in our culture: the elevation of personal feelings as the ultimate authority. Society often suggests that our internal sense of self is more trustworthy than objective truth. While feelings are powerful and meaningful, they are also temporary and can be easily influenced by external factors. Relying solely on feelings for our identity can lead us into confusion and insecurity, rather than clarity and peace.

The Truth: Feelings are important, but they're not a foundation for truth. Jeremiah 17:9 reminds us, *"The heart is deceitful above all things."* In other words, while our emotions can guide us, they shouldn't govern us. Truth isn't a feeling; it's a foundation. The Bible invites us to ground our identity not in fleeting emotions, but in the unchanging reality of God's design and love.

Feelings can change, but God's truth remains steady. When we place our trust in His design, we experience a peace that surpasses understanding, rooted not in shifting emotions but in the unshakeable foundation of His Word.

Embracing the Truth in a Confused Culture

When we confront these myths with truth, we aren't rejecting people or their experiences. Instead, we're offering a path toward lasting peace and purpose. As we navigate a culture that often strays from biological and biblical truths, we're called to bring a steady, compassionate voice, rooted in science and Scripture. This isn't about winning arguments; it's about guiding people toward the freedom of understanding who they truly are.

After examining the biblical, biological, and cultural perspectives on gender, we return to a central truth: our identity is a gift from God, meant to be received and cherished. In a world that encourages self-definition and reinvention, Christ offers us a firm foundation that does not shift with feelings or trends. In a world that questions who we are, Christ answers with clarity. Reclaiming the gift of gender isn't about restrictions; it's about embracing the intentional design God has for each of us.

Many who struggle with questions of identity often feel a deep sense of confusion, shame, or even rejection. The pain is real, and as believers, we're called to respond with compassion and understanding. Jesus Himself demonstrated love to those who felt misunderstood or marginalized, bringing healing where there was brokenness. In Christ, we find not only acceptance but restoration.

Ephesians 2:10 tells us, *"For we are God's masterpiece, created in Christ Jesus to do good works, which God prepared in advance for us to do."* This powerful truth reminds us that God's design, including our gender, is not something that needs improvement or adjustment; it is already a masterpiece. When we embrace our identity as God's masterpiece, we find peace in who we are. In reclaiming the gift of gender, we discover that our value is not in changing ourselves but in embracing the beauty of God's original plan.

Our culture often portrays God's design as restrictive, suggesting that adhering to a biblical view of gender somehow limits freedom. But Christ offers a freedom that isn't found in self-invention—it's

Discover Who You Are

found in surrendering to the Creator who knows us better than we know ourselves.

> **True freedom isn't doing whatever we want; it's living as God created us to be.**

This freedom means we no longer have to chase the world's approval or try to redefine ourselves to fit in. It frees us from the constant pressure to measure up to society's shifting standards. Jesus said in John 8:32, *"Then you will know the truth, and the truth will set you free."* When we know the truth of our God-given identity, we are liberated from the lies that tell us we need to alter or diminish ourselves to find happiness.

This truth releases us from striving, allowing us to live with the confidence that we are fully loved and fully known by our Creator.

> **In Christ, we're not just free to be ourselves; we're free to be our best selves—the selves God intended all along.**

When we reclaim our gender identity in Christ, we become living reflections of God's design. Our lives can communicate His goodness, His creativity, and His purpose to a world searching for meaning. Every time we live confidently in our God-given identity, we show the world what it looks like to live in harmony with the Creator's design.

In reclaiming gender as a gift from God, we are also invited to honor and respect the differences He established between male and female. These distinctions are not barriers; they're bridges that connect us in meaningful ways. Each of us, as men and women, contribute uniquely to the body of Christ, offering strengths that complement and support one another. When we celebrate these differences, we honor the God who created them, reflecting the unity and diversity of His design.

The beauty of reclaiming gender in Christ is that it's not an isolated journey—it's something we do in community. In the body of Christ, we are brothers and sisters, each with unique roles and purposes, designed to support, encourage, and challenge one another. Our identity in Christ connects us to a family where gender is valued and respected as part of God's beautiful plan. Together, we learn what it means to live as men and women created in His image, growing closer to Him and each other as we embrace His vision for our lives.

Reclaiming the gift of gender in Christ is an invitation to live with purpose and clarity, anchored in His unchanging truth. It's a call to step out of confusion and into the peace of knowing we are made with intention and love. We don't have to reinvent ourselves to find value; in Christ, we already have it. Our identity isn't a battle to fight; it's a gift to receive.

God's design for gender is part of a much larger picture—a picture of love, purpose, and redemption. He created us male and female, not as labels or restrictions, but as expressions of His own image. Embracing this truth allows us to live freely and confidently, knowing we are exactly who He intended us to be.

Chapter 4
Scrolling and Searching for Self

We've all been there: scrolling through social media, *"just for a minute,"* and suddenly, half an hour has disappeared. One minute we're looking up a friend's latest vacation photos, and before we know it, we're knee-deep in someone else's life, comparing their best moments with our everyday reality. How does that happen? How did I start with smoothie recipes and end up questioning my life choices? Social media has this unique power to draw us in, one perfectly filtered square at a time.

Social media isn't inherently bad; it's a tool. And like any tool, it's all about how we use it. It's where we can connect with friends, find inspiration, and share moments. But it's also a place where we see everyone else's highlight reel and, if we're not careful, start questioning our own worth in the process.

> **Comparison is easy; contentment is a choice.**

It's simple to look at someone's beautiful vacation photos, career announcements, or family updates and feel like we're falling behind. But those posts only show part of the story.

Discover Who You Are

The truth is, social media gives us glimpses, not the whole picture. It's like watching the trailer and thinking you've seen the entire movie. People post what they want us to see, not necessarily what's real. And when we start stacking up our unedited lives against these curated moments, it's easy to feel that we don't measure up.

> **We're comparing our behind-the-scenes with everyone else's highlight reel.**

Social media invites us into a world of carefully curated moments, a highlight reel that showcases the best, most polished parts of everyone's lives. Think about it: when was the last time you saw a post about someone's bad day, their doubts, or their struggles? Rarely do we get glimpses of the hard, messy moments that make up most of life. Instead, we see the award ceremony, not the long nights of hard work; the beautiful vacation, not the months of saving up.

> **We see the filter, but we miss the flaws.**

The trap of comparison is subtle. It often starts innocently enough—scrolling to catch up with friends or to find a little inspiration. But soon, we're stacking up our real lives against a lineup of *"highlight reels,"* measuring our everyday struggles

Identity Revolution

against the most beautiful, successful moments others choose to share. It's a setup that can only leave us feeling like we're falling short. When we measure our worth by likes, we lose sight of our real value.

Comparison on social media can sneak up on us because it often doesn't feel like jealousy or envy in the traditional sense. It might just feel like a passing thought: *"Wow, they're doing so well—maybe I'm not working hard enough."* Or *"Look at their family; they always seem so happy."* Without realizing it, we begin measuring our lives against snapshots of others' best moments. Comparison can make contentment feel like it's just out of reach.

Studies confirm this effect: people who frequently engage in social media often report feeling less satisfied with their own lives. Platforms like Instagram and Facebook amplify the *"fear of missing out,"* showing us glimpses of things we didn't know we wanted until we saw someone else with them. From friendships to material things to achievements, the comparison trap makes us question if we're *"enough"*—if we're successful enough, attractive enough, loved enough.

It's easy to forget that social media is not an accurate reflection of real life. People don't typically share their struggles, and even when they do, it's usually in a way that's still polished. We see filtered photos, carefully crafted captions, and sometimes even photo edits that present a version of life that's miles away from reality. We're scrolling through someone's highlight reel, not their behind-the-scenes.

Our identity isn't defined by how we compare to others, but by the truth of who we are. God doesn't look at us in comparison to anyone else; He sees us as uniquely created and fully loved in our own right. When we try to live up to someone else's carefully crafted image, we end up chasing an illusion rather than embracing the truth of who we are in Him.

Breaking free from the comparison trap begins with choosing contentment. Instead of focusing on what others have, we can choose to be grateful for what God has given us. Contentment doesn't mean we stop pursuing goals or that we give up on dreams. It simply means that we don't measure our worth by someone else's journey. True contentment isn't found in scrolling; it's found in knowing that we're exactly where God has us for a reason.

The trap of comparison is as old as humanity itself, but social media has given it a new platform. The more we understand that social media shows only fragments of people's lives, the more freedom we have to let go of comparisons. We don't need to chase after someone else's life because God has given each of us our own story, with purpose and meaning uniquely crafted for us. In the end, contentment is found not in looking outward at what others have, but in looking inward and upward, finding peace in the person God has created us to be.

The Pursuit of Validation

Social media doesn't just pull us into comparison; it pulls us into the pursuit of validation. Those little red hearts, thumbs up, and notifications are designed to give us a quick burst of satisfaction—a small affirmation that says, *"You're seen. You're liked. You're valued."* Over time, it's easy to start craving that approval, checking our phones for likes, comments, and shares. Approval might feel good, but it doesn't fulfill us.

Social media platforms are expertly designed to tap into our brain's reward system. Each time we receive a *"like"* or positive feedback, our brain releases dopamine—a chemical associated with pleasure and reward. This small dopamine hit creates a temporary sense of happiness, encouraging us to return for more. But the thrill doesn't last long, leading us to chase that feeling over and over again.

Discover Who You Are

> Living for likes can feel good for a moment, but it leaves us empty in the long run.

It's like snacking on candy: each *"like"* gives a quick burst of satisfaction, but it's not the deep nourishment our hearts truly need. When we start measuring our value by these fleeting moments of approval, we're setting ourselves up for a cycle of highs and lows, depending on the opinions of others to feel good about ourselves. This dependence on social validation can become an identity trap, pulling us away from the steady assurance of who we are in Christ.

When our worth becomes tied to social media approval, it creates an emotional rollercoaster. One moment, we feel validated by the attention, and the next, we're questioning our worth if the response isn't what we hoped. We start asking, *"Was I not interesting enough? Should I have posted a better picture? Did I say the wrong thing?"* This endless questioning can lead to feelings of inadequacy, insecurity, and even anxiety.

Psychologists have found that heavy social media use, particularly when it's focused on validation, is linked to increased feelings of depression and loneliness. People who seek affirmation online often find themselves feeling more isolated and less connected in real life. When we live for likes, we lose the freedom to live authentically.

Identity Revolution

Our desire for validation isn't wrong; it's part of being human. We all want to feel valued, appreciated, and loved. But when we look to social media for that sense of worth, we're bound to feel unsatisfied. The approval we get online is temporary, and it can never provide the deep, unconditional love we're wired to need. True validation can't be found in a scroll; it's only found in the unchanging love of God.

The solution to breaking free from this cycle of validation-seeking isn't to stop using social media entirely. It's about shifting our focus from seeking approval to living authentically. We don't need to present a perfect image to the world to feel valuable. Our worth isn't tied to how many likes we get or how well our posts perform. Instead, we're invited to live confidently in the truth that our identity is rooted in God's love.

Jesus Himself faced the temptation of public approval. People praised Him, and others rejected Him. But He remained focused on His purpose, knowing that His worth came from His relationship with the Father, not from the approval of others.

> **In a world chasing approval, Jesus calls us to live from a place of assurance.**

Discover Who You Are

Our identity isn't up for grabs every time we post a photo or share a thought. When we base our worth on God's love, we're no longer held captive by the need for social media validation. We're free to post what's real, to connect genuinely, and to live fully, knowing that we are already approved by the One who matters most. When we know we're already loved, the world's approval loses its power.

Filters and Facades – The Mask of Perfection

Social media gives us powerful tools to control how we present ourselves to the world. Filters, carefully curated photos, and edited captions allow us to create a version of ourselves that looks flawless. It's natural to want to put our best foot forward, but there's a hidden cost. The more perfect our online image, the harder it becomes to let others see who we really are.

Let's be honest—who doesn't like a good filter now and then? A little touch-up here, a better angle there. Social media has turned each of us into our own PR managers, able to adjust our *"brand"* with a swipe or tap. But the problem with perfection is that it's exhausting. When we constantly polish, edit, and filter our lives, we

> **Perfection on the outside often hides insecurity on the inside.**

Identity Revolution

start feeling the pressure to live up to this idealized version of ourselves.

Filters aren't just for photos; they're for life. We filter what we say, how we act, and even how we think about ourselves, all in an effort to maintain this *"ideal"* image. It's like wearing a mask that we've designed ourselves, and after a while, we may start forgetting what's underneath.

Creating a perfect online image can feel like a safety net—it lets us show the world the version of ourselves that we think they'll love. But this constant *"image management"* can become a trap. We start believing that if people really knew us, flaws and all, they wouldn't accept us. So, we keep the facade intact, presenting a version of ourselves that looks impressive but isn't fully authentic. When we trade honesty for approval, we miss out on genuine connection.

This mask of perfection not only distances us from others; it distances us from ourselves. We end up living in tension between who we are and who we present ourselves to be. It's like trying to balance on a tightrope—straining to keep up appearances while feeling unstable inside. Eventually, the pressure to maintain this image wears us down, making it harder and harder to feel truly known and accepted.

The Bible invites us to something radically different from the world's definition of perfection. God doesn't ask us to filter out our flaws or curate our lives to meet a certain standard. He invites us to bring our real, unfiltered selves into His presence, knowing that we are loved exactly as we are. God calls us to be real, not perfect.

In 2 Corinthians 12:9, Paul writes, *"My grace is sufficient for you, for my power is made perfect in weakness."* This truth reminds us that God isn't looking for polished perfection; He's looking for genuine hearts willing to trust Him with their flaws. When we stop hiding behind filters and facades, we give others permission to do the same, creating relationships that are built on honesty, not on image.

Breaking free from the need to appear perfect requires a shift in focus. Instead of striving for approval, we can rest in the assurance that we are fully loved by God, no filters needed. We don't have to hide our weaknesses or cover up our insecurities. In fact, our willingness to be real allows God's strength to shine through our imperfections.

When we embrace authenticity, we're no longer limited by the pressure to maintain a flawless image.

> Freedom isn't found in hiding our flaws; it's found in embracing them with grace.

We become free to share our lives openly, letting go of the mask and letting others see the person God created us to be.

As we let go of the mask of perfection, we discover a deeper connection with God and with others. We're no longer performing or pretending, but simply living in the fullness of who we are, secure in God's love and confident in His acceptance. In a world that demands perfection, God calls us to authenticity, inviting us to live boldly and without pretense.

Choosing Contentment Over Comparison

The path to reclaiming our true identity often begins by releasing the pressure to measure up to others. In a culture that constantly shows us who we *"should"* be, choosing contentment can feel countercultural. Social media gives us instant access to everyone else's accomplishments, looks, and lives, but it doesn't tell us who we are. Contentment isn't found in what we see online; it's found in knowing that we're already enough in Christ.

True contentment begins with understanding that our worth isn't determined by comparisons or validation from others; it's grounded in God's unchanging love. 1 John 3:1 says, *"See what great love the Father has lavished on us, that we should be called children of God! And that is what we are!"* This verse reminds us that our identity as

Discover Who You Are

God's children is unshakable. We don't have to earn it, and it doesn't fluctuate with opinions or trends.

Our identity in Christ is a foundation that frees us from the constant need to prove ourselves. Instead of looking to others for affirmation, we find lasting security in who God says we are. This shift takes us off the rollercoaster of comparison and places us on solid ground. When our worth is anchored in God's love, we can live freely, without the weight of needing to measure up.

Contentment doesn't mean we have to stop dreaming or striving for growth; it simply means we're not letting comparison steal our joy. One of the best ways to nurture contentment is through gratitude. When we focus on the blessings we already have, we become less focused on what we lack or what others possess.

Research even shows that practicing gratitude has mental and emotional benefits, reducing stress and increasing happiness. Each day, taking a few moments to thank God for the good things in our lives shifts our perspective from *"what's missing"* to *"what's already here."*

> **Gratitude shifts our focus from what's missing to what's already good.**

In Philippians 4:11-13, Paul speaks about learning the secret of contentment, saying, *"I have learned to be content whatever the circumstances… I can do all this through Him who gives me strength."* Paul's contentment wasn't based on his surroundings or possessions; it was based on his relationship with Christ. This kind of contentment allows us to appreciate what we have without constantly comparing ourselves to others.

When we stop chasing the world's version of success and start valuing the life God has given us, we begin to see ourselves through His eyes. Embracing our unique gifts, strengths, and even our weaknesses, we find peace in who we are.

> **Contentment is found not in what we achieve but in who we become.**

Choosing contentment over comparison means celebrating others without feeling like it takes anything away from us. We can genuinely rejoice in someone else's success, beauty, or blessings without feeling insecure because we know that God's love and purpose for us are just as profound. Each of us is created with unique gifts, designed to contribute something only we can bring to the world.

When we reclaim our identity in Christ, we let go of the comparisons that drain our joy and embrace the freedom of living authentically. We are free to be exactly who God intended us to be, without the need to edit, filter, or compare. Our worth isn't a moving target—it's grounded in the love of a God who calls us His own.

Living with Intentionality

Social media isn't going away, and it doesn't have to. It can be a powerful tool for connection, inspiration, and encouragement. But to use it without losing ourselves, we have to approach it intentionally, remembering that our identity is already complete in Christ. We're called to share light, not chase likes. When we live from a place of purpose, we can engage with social media in a way that uplifts rather than undermines our sense of self.

God has called us to be lights in this world (Matthew 5:14-16), not to seek our worth in the ever-changing opinions of others. Imagine the impact we could have if we used our online presence to reflect His love, kindness, and truth.

> **Social media can be a platform for God's truth instead of a stage for self-validation.**

When we post with purpose—whether sharing moments of gratitude, encouraging others, or simply being authentic—we allow our light to shine, showing others that they are also enough just as they are.

Remembering that our lives are about more than likes and followers helps us focus on what truly matters. Our purpose isn't measured in likes; it's measured in love. God calls us to something far greater than momentary validation; He invites us to an eternal relationship with Him, one where we are fully known and loved. When we live with this eternal perspective, we find that social media becomes less of a mirror and more of a window—a way to let God's light shine through us into the lives of others.

To keep social media in its rightful place, consider setting boundaries that protect your peace and sense of self. Intentional habits—like taking digital breaks, practicing gratitude, or setting time limits—can help create space for reflection and prayer. Invite God into the process, asking Him to reveal any areas where comparison, validation-seeking, or image management may have crept in.

Living with intentionality means using social media to connect, not to compete. When we approach social media from this perspective, it no longer controls us. Instead, it becomes a space where we share the unique story God is writing in our lives, without the need to edit or perform.

Our identity is secure, not because of what others think but because of who God says we are. We're free to be authentic, content, and confident in Him. Social media can reflect our lives, but it doesn't define them. When we're rooted in Christ, we can engage the world—including social media—with freedom, purpose, and peace.

Chapter 5
The Father Gap – Finding Identity in a World of Absence

In every family photo, there's a role that no one else can quite fill: the father. Beyond his physical presence, a father's influence brings grounding, security, and stability, shaping how we see ourselves and how we approach life's challenges. Fathers set a tone, whether intentionally or not, that gives children a framework for understanding their own value and identity. Yet, in today's world, so many of us grew up without that presence. A father's presence is more than physical; it's an anchor for identity.

For many, fatherlessness isn't just a statistic; it's a personal, silent reality that leaves an invisible mark on self-worth and identity. As children, we might not have known how to articulate the void, but we felt it deeply. A father's absence often leaves us in a quiet search—searching for approval, affirmation, and the steady hand that lets us know we're loved and valued. Without this presence, we drift, carrying questions that remain unanswered: Who am I? Am I worth anything?

Discover Who You Are

In my own life, this absence shaped me in ways I couldn't fully grasp until later. Raised by a single mother, I saw her strength and resilience—qualities I greatly admired and leaned on. But there was a part of me that always felt untethered, that grounding presence I instinctively knew was missing. Growing up without a father felt like starting a journey without a map; I was on my way, but I wasn't always sure where I was going or if I was enough to get there.

And that's the quiet ache so many of us carry—the unanswered question of who we are in the absence of a father's voice. For millions, this isn't just a story; it's a shaping force in our lives. Fatherlessness, whether by distance, neglect, or loss, leaves a space that echoes with what-ifs and why-nots. But the story doesn't end with the absence, because in that very space of loss, there is an invitation to discover a Father who never leaves.

The father gap may leave an empty space, but God's love fills it with a foundation that no one can shake. While earthly fathers may be absent, God steps into that space, offering us an identity that no one else can give or take away. In Him, we find the approval, affirmation, and security we long for—a love that heals, guides, and anchors us in ways we may have thought were lost forever.

The Fatherless Epidemic

In our society today, fatherlessness is no longer an exception; it's becoming an all-too-common experience, with profound consequences that affect not only individuals but entire communities. The numbers paint a sobering picture: One in four children in the United States grows up without a father in the home (U.S. Census Bureau). That's nearly 18 million children without the daily presence of a father figure—an absence that carries a silent but significant weight.

> When fathers are absent, the impact isn't just felt at home; it ripples through society.

Over the past few decades, the rate of fatherlessness has steadily increased, affecting people across racial, economic, and geographic lines. This rising trend is linked to a cascade of challenges that extend far beyond the household. According to the National Fatherhood Initiative, children raised in father-absent homes are:

- ***Four times more likely to live in poverty.*** The absence of a father often correlates with lower household income, increasing the risk of economic hardship.

- ***More likely to struggle academically***, with twice the risk of dropping out of high school compared to children in two-parent households (National Center for Education Statistics).
- ***At greater risk of criminal behavior***, with studies revealing that children without a father are significantly more likely to end up in the criminal justice system.

The ripple effect of fatherlessness creates a cycle of struggle that often continues across generations. Without the stability and support of a father, children are left vulnerable to an array of hardships that can follow them into adulthood. The absence of a father doesn't just leave an empty seat; it often creates a cycle of struggle that can last generations.

Fatherlessness doesn't just create economic or educational challenges; it leaves an impact that goes much deeper, touching the core of a child's identity. Studies indicate that children from father-absent homes are more likely to experience lower self-esteem, higher levels of anxiety, and increased rates of depression (American Psychological Association). This absence leads to questions that linger, questions that shape a child's internal dialogue: Am I enough? Do I matter? Am I loved?

Identity Revolution

> **The father gap leaves an empty space, one that children instinctively seek to fill.**

Without a father's steady influence, children often struggle with a sense of incompleteness, which can turn into a lifelong search for validation and belonging. A father's presence provides a model of responsibility, integrity, and strength—qualities that children look to as they develop their own sense of self. Without that model, many children are left grasping for identity, often trying to fill the void through relationships, accomplishments, or even harmful behaviors. For many, the absence of a father creates an internal drive for approval, an attempt to answer the silent question: *"Am I enough?"*

The emotional impact extends beyond childhood, often shaping how individuals approach relationships, self-worth, and resilience as adults. Research highlights that young people from fatherless homes are more prone to mental health issues, substance abuse, and difficulties forming healthy relationships (National Institutes of Health). This struggle isn't merely psychological—it's spiritual. The absence of a father figure often leaves a gap that feels irreplaceable, a longing for a steady hand that affirms and guides.

And yet, the void left by a father's absence, as deep as it may feel, is not beyond hope. God's presence is greater, filling what we thought could never be filled, providing a foundation where once there was only emptiness. In Him, there is a security that answers our questions, not with mere affirmation, but with the unchanging truth of who we are as His beloved children.

Statistics on fatherlessness give us a broad view of the impact, but for those of us who grew up without a father, it's more than just numbers—it's personal. In my single-parent home, my mother stayed with us, but she was often emotionally checked out, doing what she could to keep things together without really being there in the ways a young child needs. Her focus was survival: providing, working, and ensuring that we had food on the table. But there was a gap where nurturing and guidance should have been. Without the emotional presence of a parent who could offer both stability and encouragement, I was left to navigate life with questions that didn't have answers.

The absence of a father figure loomed like a shadow, creating a quiet space where insecurities took root. Growing up without a father felt like starting a journey without a map; I was on my way, but I wasn't always sure where I was going or if I was enough to get there.

Without a father's presence, I found myself on an unspoken search for approval, seeking validation that could somehow fill the gaps. I wanted someone to affirm me, to say, *"You're doing well. You're enough."* At the time, I didn't realize how deeply I needed this affirmation, but I was constantly striving to be noticed, hoping for the kind of encouragement that only a father's steady hand could provide. Without a father's affirmation, I felt like I was trying to complete a puzzle with missing pieces.

School wasn't the place where I found my worth. Discipline didn't come easily, and school felt like a constant struggle, something I didn't particularly enjoy or excel in. Instead, I poured myself into sports, hoping that maybe success on the field could fill the void left by my father's absence. Sports became my outlet, my place to strive for something greater, and where I hoped to gain the approval I longed for. But even with the wins, the validations were fleeting, and the emptiness remained.

The challenge of fatherlessness went beyond the absence of a male role model; it was a sense of abandonment that ran deep, a quiet feeling that maybe I wasn't worth sticking around for. This sense of being overlooked settled into my understanding of myself. Some days, I would try to convince myself I didn't need anyone's approval, that I was fine on my own. Other days, the void felt all-consuming.

In the absence of a father, I looked to others to define what it meant to be a man. I turned to older brothers and other male figures around me, piecing together an understanding of manhood from their actions and attitudes. But many of these examples fed me false identities. I saw toughness portrayed as strength, detachment as resilience, and success as the ultimate measure of worth. Without a father to ground me in a true sense of identity, I absorbed these incomplete, distorted images of manhood.

So I tried to fill the void in various ways, looking for affirmation in friendships, in relationships with girls, and even through drugs. Each of these felt, in the moment, like they could finally answer the questions I was asking. Maybe acceptance from friends would mean I was valuable, or maybe the attention from girls would give me the worth I craved. But these pursuits only offered temporary relief. When we lack a father's approval, we can find ourselves chasing validation in all the wrong places.

Growing up without a father shaped my understanding of myself, but it also left me with a deep hunger for something greater, something unshakable. When I encountered the words of the Bible describing God as a Father who is close, constant, and unwavering, it was like water to a desert. Unlike the examples I'd grown up with, here was a Father who didn't just exist at a distance or require me to prove my worth. He knew me completely, loved me fully, and called me His own. To see myself as God sees me was to find the approval I had searched for in every other place.

Scripture revealed a Father who *"takes great delight"* in His children, who *"rejoices over you with si*nging" (Zephaniah 3:17).

Identity Revolution

The words of Psalm 139 assured me that He not only knows me but has searched my heart, that He is *"familiar with all my* ways" and has *"woven me together in my mother's womb."* This kind of intimate love was beyond anything I had experienced; every verse was like a reminder that God saw me as precious, known, and loved beyond measure.

Reading about God's love—His acceptance, His faithfulness, His intimate knowledge of my heart—began to fill the empty spaces left by my earthly father's absence. Isaiah 43:1 says, *"Do not fear, for I have redeemed you; I have called you by name; you are mine."* Each verse that spoke of His commitment, His sacrifice, and His delight in His children felt like a balm, healing the insecurities and questions I'd carried for so long. In God's eyes, I wasn't someone striving to measure up; I was a beloved child, worthy and whole.

The Father's love is steadfast and unbreakable, as Romans 8:38-39 reminds us that *"neither death nor life, neither angels nor demons, neither the present nor the future...will be able to separate us from the love of God that is in Christ Jesus our Lord."* Every passage that spoke of this kind of love was a revelation. In His words, I found a Father who was everything I'd been searching for—a love that needed no performance, a security that wouldn't fade.

This realization didn't just change how I saw myself; it changed how I saw my life. In God, I discovered an identity that was secure, a love that was steadfast, and a purpose grounded not in what I could achieve but in who He made me to be.

The Biblical View of God as Father

In a world where earthly fathers can be absent, distant, or imperfect, God steps into that gap as the perfect Father. The Bible describes Him as a *"Father to the fatherless"* (Psalm 68:5), a title that speaks directly to those of us who have felt the emptiness left by an absent or emotionally distant father. God's presence isn't like any other; He doesn't just fill the void of a human father—He transforms it, bringing healing and a sense of belonging that goes beyond anything the world can offer.

> In a world of absence, God is present, offering us an identity rooted in His perfect love.

But to truly experience God as our Father, we must confront and dismantle our distorted perspectives of Him. Often, we view God through the lens of our earthly fathers, transferring human limitations and failings onto Him. This can lead to deeply ingrained, but inaccurate, images of who He is.

Common Misconceptions About God as Father

1. The Absent Father

Some of us grew up with fathers who were physically or emotionally absent, leaving us to fend for ourselves in moments when we desperately needed guidance and support. This experience can lead us to see God as distant, unavailable, or uninterested in the details of our lives. But Scripture reveals a different story. God says in Deuteronomy 31:6, *"I will never leave you nor forsake you."* Far from being absent, God promises His constant presence.

> **When earthly fathers walk away, God steps in to stay.**

2. The Judgmental Father

For others, the experience of a father may have been one of harsh criticism and constant judgment, feeling that they could never measure up. This image can color our view of God, making us see Him as an exacting judge who's never quite pleased with us. However, Romans 8:1 assures us, *"There is now no condemnation for those who are in Christ Jesus."* God's heart is not to condemn but to love, correct, and guide us in grace.

> Where judgment may have marked our past, grace now defines our present.

3. The Conditional Father

Some grew up with fathers whose love felt conditional, given only when we succeeded or met certain standards. This can make us feel that we have to earn God's love through perfection or achievement. But Jeremiah 31:3 tells us of God's unconditional love: "*I have loved you with an everlasting love; I have drawn you with unfailing kindness.*" God's love isn't dependent on our performance; it is steadfast and freely given.

> With God as our Father, love is not a reward; it's a guarantee.

4. The Passive Father

Others may have had fathers who were physically present but emotionally uninvolved, offering little guidance, discipline, or engagement. This can lead us to see God as passive, indifferent, or

Identity Revolution

uninvolved in our personal struggles. Yet, the Bible describes a Father who is intimately aware of every detail of our lives. In Psalm 139, David speaks of a God who knows us completely, who *"knit*

> God isn't just aware of us; He is deeply invested in every part of our journey.

[us] together in [our] mother's womb" (Psalm 139:13). God's involvement in our lives is personal, attentive, and intentional.

5. The Angry Father

For those who grew up with fathers who expressed anger more than love, the idea of God as Father may be clouded by fear. This perspective can make us hesitant to approach God, fearing we'll provoke His wrath or disappointment. But Psalm 103:8 tells us, *"The Lord is compassionate and gracious, slow to anger, abounding in love."* God's anger is righteous, but it is tempered by His compassion, mercy, and understanding.

> God's primary posture toward us is love, not anger.

84

God as the Perfect Father

Understanding God as our true Father means re-learning what fatherhood can look like in its perfection. God's role as a Father isn't just a comforting metaphor; it's a profound reality that brings clarity to our identity and purpose. Where earthly fathers may have fallen short, God remains steady—a source of unwavering love, guidance, and acceptance.

In 2 Corinthians 6:18, God makes a powerful promise: *"I will be a Father to you, and you will be my sons and daughters."* This isn't conditional on our achievements or performance; it's a promise of belonging that is eternal. With God as our Father, we are no longer abandoned or overlooked; we are chosen and fully known.

Unlike human relationships, which can feel conditional, God's love for us is constant. He doesn't withdraw His love when we fall short, nor does He abandon us in moments of weakness. His love is patient and enduring, surpassing any earthly standard of fatherhood.

> In a life filled with conditional love, God's love remains the one thing we don't have to earn.

As I began to understand God's role as my Father, my understanding of myself started to change. The insecurities that stemmed from fatherlessness—feelings of not being enough or not being wanted—began to lose their hold. Knowing that God is a Father who delights in me and who calls me by name reshaped my view of who I am. Our identity is grounded in the reality that we are not orphans but beloved children.

God's love isn't based on our performance or success; it's rooted in His character as a Father. In moments of doubt, I could look to Him and find reassurance, knowing that my identity was grounded in His unchanging acceptance. His presence and affirmation offer a security that doesn't waver with circumstances or fade with time. With God as our Father, we find a love that doesn't waver, a foundation that doesn't shake.

For anyone who has felt the ache of fatherlessness, embracing God as Father offers a path to healing and restoration. He doesn't just cover up the gaps left by an earthly father's absence; He fills them with His presence, reshaping our identity from the inside out. Where earthly fathers may have failed to love, protect, or affirm us, God steps in with a love that is unconditional, a presence that is constant, and a commitment that is eternal.

The journey to see God as our true Father can transform our lives. As we shed the distorted perspectives of who we thought He was, we begin to see Him as He truly is—a Father who loves, cares, and knows us fully.

> **With Him, we don't just find a Father; we find the foundation of who we are.**

Discovering God as our Father is more than a comfort; it's the start of a profound healing journey, one that leads us from brokenness to wholeness. When we allow God's love to fill the empty spaces left by fatherlessness, our identity begins to transform. The weight of abandonment, the endless search for approval—these burdens start to fall away. Instead, we build our sense of self on a foundation that is unshakeable, grounded in the knowledge that we are fully loved, fully accepted, and fully known. Healing comes when we allow God to be the Father who never leaves and never fails.

For those of us shaped by the absence of a father, healing isn't an overnight fix. It's a process—one that involves unlearning old patterns and learning to accept love without strings attached. God offers us the chance to rewrite the narratives we've carried—narratives that once told us we weren't enough or that we had to earn love. Through Christ, we're invited into a new story, one where our worth isn't based on what we lack but on what we have in Him.

In 2 Corinthians 5:17, we read, *"Therefore, if anyone is in Christ, the new creation has come: The old has gone, the new is here!"* This verse captures the heart of our transformation. We're no longer defined by the wounds of our past, by the abandonment we may have felt, or by the insecurities we carried. Instead, we become new creations, shaped by God's unchanging love and strengthened by His presence. In Christ, we don't just find healing; we find a new identity, whole and complete.

As God rebuilds our identity, we begin to walk in a new confidence—a confidence grounded in the assurance that we are loved, valued, and called by Him. This doesn't mean we'll never face insecurities, but it does mean we now have a foundation that can withstand them. When doubts arise, we can return to the truth of who we are in God: a beloved child with a purpose.

The journey from fatherlessness to wholeness isn't just about personal healing; it's about stepping into a life of purpose. The void left by an earthly father becomes a space filled with God's calling for our lives. Where we once questioned our worth, we now find strength, knowing that God sees us as uniquely valuable, worthy of love, and capable of making an impact.

> **Our earthly experiences may shape us, but our identity in Christ defines us.**

Choosing to live authentically in the identity God has given us takes courage. It means stepping out from behind the masks and labels we've learned to wear. It means rejecting the lies we've been told and the ones we've told ourselves. This kind of authenticity isn't about being *"real"* in a superficial way; it's about being true to who God created us to be. True identity isn't found in the layers we add; it's found in the truth that remains when we let God shape who we are.

Claiming our true identity is both an act of faith and an act of freedom. It's a decision to live fully as the person God designed, unshaken by the shifting opinions of others and unfazed by our own insecurities. To embrace this identity is to step into a life of purpose, anchored in a security that doesn't depend on our achievements or the approval of others. We're invited to live as God's beloved children, chosen and cherished, uniquely called to impact the world.

God's love isn't just a balm for our wounds; it's the foundation for who we are and who we're becoming. As we walk forward, we step into the fullness of this truth, ready to live whole, loved, and secure in God's hands. This isn't the end of a journey but the beginning of a life fully grounded in the identity God has intended for us from the start.

21 DAY
DEVOTION

Discovering Your Identity in Christ

Day 1: Created in God's Image

Memory Verse

> *"So, God created mankind in his own image, in the image of God he created them; male and female he created them."*
>
> *Genesis 1:27 (NIV)*

It's easy to let the world shape how we see ourselves. Everywhere we turn, there's a subtle (or not-so-subtle) voice telling us what we should look like, act like, or achieve in order to be *"someone."* Maybe it's the person who seems to have it all together on social media, or that polished image we've built over time to fit in with the crowd. But here's the question: are we truly who we think we are, or have we just bought into an identity that was sold to us by culture, insecurity, or even past wounds?

The truth is, we can easily define ourselves by how we look, our accomplishments, or what others say about us. But if we allow that, we're placing our identity on shaky ground—because trends change, accomplishments fade, and opinions shift like the wind. Instead, there's a deeper, unshakable identity that was woven into us from the moment God breathed life into us. Genesis 1:27 tells us that we are made in the very image of God. Not kind of like God. Not a watered-down version of Him. We were created to reflect Him in every way. That's the real mirror we should be looking into.

Still, if we're honest, it's tough to always believe that. Many of us struggle to see ourselves as image-bearers of the Creator. We focus on our flaws, imperfections, and past mistakes, convincing ourselves that maybe God made a mistake. But let me stop you right there:

Discover Who You Are

> **God doesn't make mistakes—only masterpieces.**

You're not the exception to that. If you feel like you don't measure up, remember this: God measured you out when He formed you, and He was pleased with the result.

You Are Made in God's Image

We live in a culture that screams, "*You are what you see!*"—as if the reflection in the mirror is the beginning and end of our identity. But you aren't the sum of your physical appearance, your status, or even your accomplishments. When God said, "*Let us make man in our image,*" He wasn't talking about our outward appearance. He was speaking to our very essence—the core of who we are. You were made to reflect His character, His creativity, and His purpose. And that, my friend, is far more valuable than anything the world can put a price tag on.

Being made in God's image means we carry divine potential. Think about that. When you look at yourself, you're not just seeing a body—you're seeing someone created to represent God's love, wisdom, and purpose on earth. You reflect His creativity every time you step into a role that requires ingenuity or compassion. You reflect His relational nature every time you reach out to love and care for others. You reflect His purpose each time you live with intention, knowing that you're not just passing through life, you're passing on God's glory.

But here's where things get tricky. The world, the enemy, and even our minds will challenge this truth. *"You're not good enough." "You're too flawed to reflect God." "You're just another face in the crowd."* These are the lies that sneak into our hearts when we start measuring ourselves by worldly standards.

> The enemy's greatest tool is to distort your identity, because if he can confuse you about who you are, he can distract you from what you're called to do.

He loves to whisper, *"You're just a product of your circumstances,"* but God's Word shouts, *"You're a product of My craftsmanship."* Don't let the noise of the world drown out the truth of God's voice.

I Am What I See

Being made in the image of God means that you're not just a reflection—you're a carrier of His presence. Just like a photo captures an image but also tells a story, your life tells a story of

Discover Who You Are

God's grace, goodness, and glory. You are a living, breathing testimony of His power. But the question is: are we reflecting that? It's one thing to know that we're made in His image, but are we living in a way that reflects His nature?

The first thing to understand about being made in God's image is that you're not a carbon copy of the world around you—you're a divine original. Think of it this way: the world may try to copy and paste its version of *"success"* or *"beauty"* onto you, but God didn't use a template when He made you; He used His own hands. And when God creates something, He doesn't just call it good, He calls it His.

This divine image-bearing also means we were made for relationship. God, in His very essence, is relational. The Father, Son, and Holy Spirit existed in perfect unity before creation ever began. When He created us in His image, He stamped that same need for connection into our souls. That's why we crave meaningful relationships, whether with God or others. We weren't designed to do life alone—whether that's in our faith journey or our personal lives. And honestly, that's a relief, because isolation was never part of the design.

The Power of Being Image-Bearers

Knowing you are made in God's image is a powerful truth, but it's even more powerful when you live like it. Reflecting God's nature isn't reserved for spiritual moments—it's seen in how you treat others, how you use your gifts, and how you see yourself. Let's explore what it means to fully embrace and embody the image of God in your daily life.

1. *You Reflect God's Creativity*

If God is the ultimate artist, you are His masterpiece (Ephesians 2:10). Just like an artist leaves a bit of themselves in every creation, you carry a piece of God's creativity in everything you do. Whether you're building a project, solving a problem, or simply being kind, you're showing the world a glimpse of your Maker. Next time you doubt your creativity, remember that you reflect the God who spoke the universe into existence. Creativity runs in your veins—God made sure of it.

2. *You Were Designed for Relationship*

God didn't create you to just exist; He made you for deep connection—with Him and with others. Being made in His image means we reflect His relational nature. No wonder we crave relationships! It's not just because we need someone to binge-watch Netflix with; it's because we were wired for connection.

> **Loneliness and isolation aren't part of God's original design.**

3. You Have a God-Given Purpose

There's nothing accidental about your existence.

> **God made you for a purpose, to live out His will on earth.**

You are on assignment! Every day is an opportunity to reflect His glory in the way you live, love, and lead. When you walk into a room, you're not just bringing yourself—you're carrying the presence of God with you! So the next time you're tempted to blend in or shrink back, remember: You were made to stand out because God made you.

Prayer

"Lord, thank You for creating me in Your image. I confess that I've allowed the world and its lies to shape how I see myself, but today I choose to stand in the truth of who You say I am. Help me to reflect Your love, creativity, and purpose in everything I do. Give me the strength to reject the lies that try to define me and to live as the masterpiece You've called me to be. Amen."

Reflection Questions

1. How have you let the world's standards shape your view of yourself?

2. What relationships in your life need more of God's image reflected in them?

3. What specific purpose do you believe God has given you? How can you start living with more intention to reflect His glory in your daily life?

Day 2: New Creation in Christ

Memory Verse

> "Therefore, if anyone is in Christ, he is a new creation. The old has passed away; behold, the new has come."
>
> 2 Corinthians 5:17 (ESV)

Discover Who You Are

If you've ever tried to reinvent yourself, you know it's not as easy as switching up your wardrobe or moving to a new city. You can change your location, job, or hairstyle, but those things don't alter who you truly are on the inside. Sometimes we think a fresh start is about wiping the slate clean ourselves, but in reality, the slate isn't just dirty—it's cracked and broken. No amount of scrubbing can fix that.

The problem is, we often try to shape our identity by our own efforts—whether it's by proving ourselves, outrunning our past, or pretending we've got it all together. But here's the truth:

> **You can't become who God created you to be by relying on who you used to be.**

It's impossible. The old you doesn't have what it takes to build the new you. That's why God doesn't just give us a makeover—He makes us new creations in Christ. And that's where the transformation begins.

You Are a New Creation in Christ

Identity Revolution

This isn't some spiritual version of a *"glow-up"* where you look a little shinier on the outside but remain the same on the inside. God doesn't work like that. He doesn't take the broken pieces of your life and just glue them back together—He gives you a brand-new heart, a new spirit, and a new identity. That's what it means to be a new creation in Christ.

When Paul says, *"The old has passed away; behold, the new has come,"* he's not talking about minor upgrades—this is a full-blown transformation. The past no longer defines you. You don't have to carry the weight of your old mistakes, regrets, or failures because God has removed that baggage. What once held you down has no power over you anymore. You've been given a fresh start in Christ, and no one can take that away.

But here's the catch: we often forget this truth. We slip back into our old habits and mindsets, believing the lie that nothing has really changed. That's where the struggle begins. The enemy loves to remind you of the *"old you,"* but Christ says, *"That's not who you are anymore."* If you're in Christ, your old self is gone—buried, done with. You are new. It's not about becoming a better version of the old you; it's about walking in the identity God has already given you.

I Am Who I Used to Be

One of the greatest traps we fall into is believing that we're still the same person we were before we met Christ. We look at ourselves through the lens of our past mistakes, habits, or even the labels others put on us. *"You're still that angry person." "You'll never overcome that sin." "This is just who you are."* Those are the lies that keep us stuck in a false identity.

But here's the truth: The old you is gone. When you accepted Christ, your past was wiped clean, and a new life began. Yet, we often live like nothing changed. We cling to old identities because they feel familiar, even if they don't bring freedom. The enemy thrives in this space—he'll whisper, *"You're no different. God hasn't really changed you."* But Christ's Word says otherwise. You are not who you used to be. God didn't just tweak a few things—He completely transformed you from the inside out.

Walking in Your New Identity

Being a new creation in Christ isn't just a spiritual truth to know—it's a reality we are called to live out daily. This new identity affects how we think, act, and respond to the world around us. But stepping into this identity requires intentional choices and practical steps. Let's look at how you can start living in the fullness of your new life today.

1. Leave the Old Behind

This might sound simple, but it's a daily choice. Walking in your new identity means leaving behind the old way of thinking, reacting, and living. It's a decision to reject the lies of your past and step into the truth of who God says you are.

> **You can't embrace your future while holding onto your past.**

If you're still carrying guilt or shame from the old you, lay it down at the cross. It's no longer yours to carry.

2. Renew Your Mind

Becoming a new creation doesn't mean you automatically think like one. Your mind has been trained by the world, but now it needs to be renewed by the Word of God (Romans 12:2). Take the time to fill your heart and mind with scripture that reminds you of your new identity. The more you renew your mind, the more your actions will align with your new life. Think of it as rewiring your brain to match the new creation that you are.

3. Live by Faith, Not by Feelings

There will be days when you don't feel like a new creation. The enemy will remind you of old failures, and your emotions may try

> **Feelings change, but God's truth remains.**

to convince you that nothing has changed. But being a new creation isn't about feelings—it's about faith.

Walk by faith, believing that the work Christ began in you is real and ongoing, even when it doesn't feel like it.

Prayer

"Lord, thank You for making me a new creation in Christ. I confess that I often fall back into old ways of thinking and living, but today I choose to embrace the new identity You've given me. Help me to walk by faith and not by feelings, and to renew my mind daily with Your truth. Thank You for the freedom and transformation You've brought into my life. In Jesus' name, Amen."

Reflection Questions

1. What old habits or mindsets are you still holding onto that don't reflect your new identity in Christ?

2. How can you actively renew your mind to align more with the truth of being a new creation?

3. What does walking by faith look like for you in this season of life, especially when you don't *"feel"* new?

Day 3: Children of God

Memory Verse

> "See how very much our Father loves us, for he calls us his children, and that is what we are! But the people who belong to this world don't recognize that we are God's children because they don't know him."
>
> 1 John 3:1 (NLT)

Discover Who You Are

If someone asked you to describe yourself, what would you say? Most of us would jump to the obvious answers: job titles, roles we play, or characteristics we display. *"I'm a teacher, a parent, a business owner."* But those descriptions only scratch the surface. Who we truly are goes far deeper than our responsibilities, talents, or personality traits. And while the world might try to slap labels on us—successful, failure, good enough, not enough—none of these really get to the heart of our identity.

The Bible says we are something far more profound: children of God. Let that sink in for a moment. You're not just an employee, friend, or parent. You're a son or daughter of the Creator of the universe. You belong to His family, which means His love, care, and purpose are poured into your life in ways we often forget to recognize. So, why do we tend to overlook this most important part of our identity?

Perhaps it's because the world is loud, constantly defining us by what we do instead of who we are. In the race to achieve, to belong, or to measure up, we can lose sight of the quiet truth that God has already declared over us: *"You are mine."* When we live defined by His declaration, rather than the world's expectations, we find freedom, purpose, and security in our identity as His children.

> **Your worth isn't found in the labels others give you; it's rooted in the love God has for you.**

You Are a Child of God

Being a child of God means that you have an intimate, personal relationship with the Father. This isn't about distant reverence or a formal religious position. It's about being known, loved, and accepted by the One who formed you. And unlike human relationships where love can be conditional, God's love for you as His child is unconditional—unchanging and unwavering.

Here's what's even more incredible: You didn't have to earn your place in God's family. He chose you. Before you were born, before you did anything right or wrong, He set His love on you and called you His own. And this is where many of us struggle. We're used to earning approval, affection, and acceptance in this world, so it feels unnatural to simply receive the identity of being God's child without proving ourselves first.

But that's the beauty of grace.

> **You are loved by God not because of what you've done, but because of who He is.**

He doesn't need a reason to love you—He already does. Just as a loving father doesn't wait for his child to "*deserve*" his love, God has always had a heart full of love for you. You are not a child who has to constantly strive for acceptance. You already belong.

I Have to Earn My Place

Despite knowing we are children of God, there's often a lingering feeling that we need to earn our place. We tell ourselves we have to perform perfectly, behave flawlessly, or meet some impossible standard to maintain God's approval. This is a trap that robs us of the joy and freedom of simply being His.

The world teaches that you only get what you deserve, but God's kingdom flips that upside down. You are His child, not because of what you've done, but because of who He is. Yet, many of us live like we're on trial, waiting for God to decide if we're worth keeping around. That's a false belief rooted in fear and performance, not in the love of the Father.

Here's the truth: God's love for you isn't fragile. It's not based on your performance or your perfection. It's based on His character. He is a good Father who delights in you, even in your weaknesses, because you're His.

Embracing Your Identity as a Child of God

It's easy to forget what it really means to be called a child of God. This isn't just a label we wear; it's a reality that should change the way we experience every aspect of life. Let's dive deeper into how this truth can bring freedom and purpose as you fully embrace your identity as God's beloved.

1. Live in Confidence, Not in Fear

Being a child of God means you can live with confidence, knowing that you are secure in His love. Fear has no place in the heart of someone who knows they are loved unconditionally. The next time you feel unworthy or uncertain of God's love, remind yourself: You belong to Him, and nothing can take that away. You don't have to live like an orphan trying to earn a home. You already have one.

2. Approach God with Boldness

As God's child, you have direct access to Him. You don't need to hesitate or wonder if you're *"good enough"* to come to Him. He invites you to approach Him boldly, just like a child who runs into the arms of their Father. Hebrews 4:16 says, *"Let us then approach God's throne of grace with confidence..."* You don't have to tiptoe around God—He welcomes you with open arms every time.

3. Reflect the Father's Heart

Children naturally reflect the traits of their parents. As a child of God, you have the privilege of reflecting His heart to the world. This means showing love, grace, and compassion to others the way He shows it to you. When you live like God's child, people should see a glimpse of the Father in you. How can you reflect His love today in the way you treat those around you?

Prayer

"Father, thank You for calling me Your child. I confess that I sometimes feel like I need to earn Your love or approval, but today I choose to rest in the truth that I am already Yours. Help me to live confidently in my identity as Your son/daughter, knowing that Your love for me never changes. Let me reflect Your heart to those around me, that they may see Your love through me. In Jesus' name, Amen."

Reflection Questions

1. How does knowing you are a child of God change the way you see yourself?

2. Are there areas in your life where you still feel like you have to earn God's approval or love?

3. How can you reflect the heart of the Father in your relationships with others this week?

Day 4: Ambassadors of Christ

Memory Verse

> "We are therefore Christ's ambassadors, as though God were making his appeal through us. We implore you on Christ's behalf: Be reconciled to God."
>
> 2 Corinthians 5:20 (NIV)

Discover Who You Are

If you've ever been asked to represent someone—maybe to speak on their behalf or deliver a message—you know the weight that comes with that responsibility. There's pressure to get the words right, to be faithful to the intent, and to make sure the message is received well. Now imagine you've been given the highest calling of all: to represent Jesus Himself to the world. It's not just a Sunday job or something for church leaders—it's the identity of every believer.

But here's the thing: many of us feel unqualified to represent Christ. We think, *"I'm not a pastor or a Bible scholar,"* or *"I don't have it all together."* The truth is, being Christ's ambassador isn't about having all the answers or living perfectly. It's about being willing to represent Him—mess and all—because

> **God's message doesn't need a perfect messenger. It needs a willing one.**

You Are Christ's Ambassador

Identity Revolution

> Your life is the letter God is sending to the world. The question is: what's being written through you?

An ambassador carries the message, values, and authority of the one they represent. You, as a follower of Christ, are called to do just that. Every conversation you have, every action you take, and every choice you make has the potential to reflect Christ to others.

Being an ambassador isn't just about knowing the gospel, it's about living it. It's about letting your life shine as an example of God's grace and truth. People may never pick up a Bible, but they are reading the way you live every day. Are they seeing a reflection of Christ in you? Are they witnessing the love, forgiveness, and peace that comes from knowing Him?

Here's the challenge: we often feel like we need to be more prepared or have a deeper understanding before we can represent Christ well. But God never waits for perfection. He chooses willing vessels, not polished ones. He's not asking you to be a spiritual expert; He's asking you to carry His message in the way you live and love.

I'm Not Qualified to Represent Christ

Discover Who You Are

The enemy loves to plant seeds of doubt when it comes to representing Christ. *"Who are you to speak for Him? You don't know enough. You've messed up too many times."* Sound familiar? But here's the truth:

> **God doesn't call the qualified; He qualifies the called.**

And you have been called.

Paul, the man who wrote most of the New Testament, didn't start out as the ideal candidate. He persecuted Christians! But once he encountered Christ, his life became a living testament to God's grace. In the same way, your qualifications don't come from you—they come from Christ working through you. It's not about your ability; it's about His power.

The moment you accepted Christ, you were given the authority to represent Him. Don't let fear or feelings of inadequacy keep you from stepping into your calling. The world needs to hear the message of reconciliation, and God has chosen you to carry it.

Living as an Ambassador of Christ

Representing Christ as His ambassador is not just a responsibility—it's a privilege. But it also requires intentionality. You're not just speaking words; you're living out the message of reconciliation to those around you. Let's explore how to faithfully carry Christ's message in your daily life.

1. Speak with Grace and Truth

As Christ's representative, your words carry weight. When you speak, people are listening to see if your life matches your message. Speak with grace, but don't shy away from the truth. An ambassador doesn't change the message to make it easier to hear—they deliver it faithfully. Make sure your words reflect the heart of Christ, full of love but also anchored in truth.

2. Reflect Christ's Love in Action

Actions speak louder than words. People might not remember everything you say, but they will remember how you made them feel. Are your actions aligning with the message of the gospel? As an ambassador of Christ, your life should be marked by love, generosity, and kindness. People may doubt what you say, but they will see what you do.

Discover Who You Are

3. Stay Connected to Your Source

No ambassador acts on their own. They stay in close communication with the one they represent. For you, this means staying connected to Christ through prayer, scripture, and worship.

> The more time you spend with Jesus, the better you'll represent Him to the world.

Don't try to carry the message on your own strength—lean into God's guidance every step of the way.

Prayer

"Lord, thank You for the incredible privilege of being Your ambassador. I confess that I sometimes feel unqualified or unsure, but I choose to trust that You've called me for this purpose. Help me to speak with grace, act with love, and stay connected to You so that my life reflects Your heart. Let everything, I do and say point others to You. In Jesus' name, Amen."

Reflection Questions

1. What does being an ambassador for Christ look like in your everyday life?

2. Are there areas in your life where your actions don't align with the message of the gospel?

3. How can you stay better connected to Christ, so you can represent Him well in both word and action?

Day 5: Chosen and Royal Priesthood

Memory Verse

"But you are a chosen people, a royal priesthood, a holy nation, God's special possession, that you may declare the praises of him who called you out of darkness into his wonderful light."

1 Peter 2:9 (NIV)

Let's face it, most of us spend our lives waiting to be chosen. Whether it's for a job, a team, or even a relationship, there's a longing in all of us to be picked. It feels good to be wanted, right? But what happens when the world overlooks us? What about the times when we feel like we're standing on the sidelines, waiting for someone—anyone—to recognize our worth?

> **You weren't chosen to sit on the bench; you were chosen to step into the role God created specifically for you.**

Here's the truth that changes everything: You've already been chosen. Not by a company or a person, but by God Himself. You are part of His royal priesthood, handpicked by the King of Kings. And that's not just a title—it's an identity that carries incredible purpose.

You Are Chosen and Royal

Being chosen by God means you're not just another face in the crowd. You're royalty. And not just any royalty—a royal priesthood. This is a big deal! In ancient times, the role of a priest was to represent the people to God and bring God's presence to the people. The priest stood in the gap, offering sacrifices and prayers on behalf of others.

Now, through Jesus, you've been given that same privilege. You no longer need someone to stand between you and God—you have direct access to the Father. You've been chosen to represent Him on earth, to be a light in the darkness, and to offer spiritual sacrifices of praise and service. It's not a duty; it's a divine calling.

But here's the part we often forget: being chosen means being set apart.

> It's easy to get caught up in the routines of life and forget that we've been called to live differently.

As part of God's royal priesthood, we're meant to stand out, not because of how great we are, but because of how great He is in us. The world may overlook you, but God sees you as His special possession, chosen for a purpose.

I'm Not Special

One of the lies we often believe is that we're not special enough to be chosen by God. We see our flaws, our failures, and our weaknesses, and we think, *"Surely God has better options than me."*

Discover Who You Are

The enemy loves to whisper this lie in your ear, hoping you'll doubt your worth and sit on the sidelines.

But here's the thing: God didn't choose you because you were perfect—He chose you because He's perfect.

> His choosing you has nothing to do with your qualifications and everything to do with His

When He picked you for His royal priesthood, He knew exactly who you were—flaws and all—and He still called you His own. You're not chosen because of what you bring to the table; you're chosen because of what He brings to your life.

So the next time you feel like you're not enough, remind yourself: You are chosen, not by accident, but with purpose.

Living as a Royal Priesthood

Being chosen by God isn't just something to know in your head; it's a reality meant to shape how you live every single day. You were called for a reason, set apart for something bigger than yourself. The question is, how will you let this truth impact your actions, your choices, and the way you represent Christ?

1. Embrace Your Role

> You weren't chosen to sit still—you were chosen to stand up.

Being chosen as part of God's royal priesthood isn't just a title you wear—it's a role you live out. This means stepping into your calling with confidence, knowing that God has equipped you for the task.

Whether it's serving in your church, sharing the gospel, or simply loving others well, embrace the calling God has placed on your life.

2. Walk in Your Authority

Royalty comes with authority. As part of God's royal family, you have been given authority through Christ. This means you don't have to walk through life feeling powerless. You've been given spiritual authority to pray, to serve, and to speak the truth in love. Don't underestimate the power you carry as a royal priest. Walk in it with boldness.

3. Declare His Praises

The most powerful thing you can do as part of God's chosen people is declare His praises. You've been called out of darkness and into

Discover Who You Are

His light, not just for your own benefit but so that others may see the glory of God through your life. When you live in gratitude and praise, you reflect the goodness of God to the world. It's not about being perfect; it's about pointing others to the One who is.

Prayer

"Father, thank You for choosing me as part of Your royal priesthood. I confess that I sometimes feel unworthy or unsure of my place in Your plan, but I choose to trust in Your calling. Help me to walk in the authority You've given me and to declare Your praises with boldness. Let my life reflect the light of Christ in everything I do. In Jesus' name, Amen."

Reflection Questions

1. What does it mean to you to be part of God's royal priesthood?

2. Are there areas in your life where you're doubting God's choice to use you?

3. How can you step into your role and walk in the spiritual authority God has given you?

Day 6: God's Masterpiece

Memory verse

> "For we are God's masterpiece. He has created us anew in Christ Jesus, so we can do the good things he planned for us long ago."
>
> Ephesians 2:10 (NLT)

Discover Who You Are

We live in a world obsessed with perfection. Social media feeds are full of picture-perfect moments, carefully filtered and curated to look flawless. It's easy to fall into the trap of thinking that we have to live up to these impossible standards. But here's the problem: perfection isn't achievable. And guess what?

> **God never asked you to be perfect—He already calls you His masterpiece.**

When God looks at you, He doesn't see your mistakes, failures, or imperfections. He sees His finest work, created with love and care. The world may try to convince you that you're not enough, but God says, *"You are My work of art."*

In a culture that constantly demands more—more achievement, more beauty, more success—it's easy to feel like we'll never measure up. But here's the amazing truth: God's standards are not the world's standards. While the world demands perfection, God delights in progress. He isn't looking for flawless performances or unattainable ideals; He's looking at your heart. In His eyes, you are already enough, not because of what you do, but because of who you are—a masterpiece shaped by the hands of the Creator.

You Are God's Masterpiece

A masterpiece isn't mass-produced. It's one-of-a-kind, painstakingly crafted by the artist's hand. That's who you are to God—His masterpiece, uniquely designed with a specific purpose in mind. When Ephesians 2:10 says you are God's masterpiece, it's not just saying you're a good idea. It's saying you are His greatest work, created in Christ Jesus for a mission.

The enemy loves to whisper that you're not special—that you're just one more person trying to make it through life. But God sees something different. He sees someone He took time to form, detail by detail. Every part of who you are—your gifts, your personality, even your quirks—was intentional.

> **You are a divine original, designed not just for existence but for purpose.**

The thing about masterpieces is that they aren't created to sit on a shelf collecting dust. They're meant to be seen, appreciated, and shared with the world. God created you to live out the good works He planned for you long ago. You are here for a purpose, and it's time to embrace the fact that you are not a mistake. You are exactly who God made you to be.

I'm Not Good Enough

One of the biggest lies we wrestle with is the belief that we're not good enough. Whether it's comparing ourselves to others or feeling like we've fallen short of our potential, the voice of inadequacy can be loud. But here's the truth:

> God didn't make a mistake when He made you. You are His masterpiece, flaws and all.

It's easy to feel like we're missing something—that we're not as talented, smart, or successful as we should be. But this mindset overlooks the fact that God has already equipped you with everything you need to fulfill the purpose He has for you. The lie that you're *"not enough"* is an attack on the masterpiece that God has already declared *"very good."*

Living as God's Masterpiece

Understanding that you are God's masterpiece changes everything. It shifts the way you see yourself and the way you live out your purpose. You are not a random collection of talents or traits—you were carefully crafted by the Creator for a reason. Let's discover how this truth can reshape your view of yourself and how you live.

Identity Revolution

1. Stop Comparing, Start Celebrating

It's easy to fall into the comparison trap, constantly measuring yourself against others. But comparing yourself to others robs you of the joy of being uniquely you.

> You're not meant to be a copy of anyone else—you're God's original masterpiece.

Instead of comparing, start celebrating the unique qualities God has placed in you. Embrace what makes you different.

2. Embrace Your Purpose

You weren't created to live without direction. God has a plan for your life, filled with good works that He specifically designed for you. Step into that purpose with confidence, knowing that God has crafted you for something meaningful. You are here for more than just going through the motions. Seek out the ways you can use your gifts to impact others and glorify God.

3. See Yourself Through God's Eyes

It's easy to be your own worst critic. We tend to focus on our shortcomings and imperfections, but God sees you through the lens of love and purpose. When you look in the mirror, remind yourself that you are looking at God's masterpiece. You are His work of art, created with intention, and designed to reflect His glory.

Prayer

"Lord, thank You for making me Your masterpiece. I confess that I've often doubted my worth and compared myself to others, but today I choose to believe what You say about me. Help me to embrace my purpose, use my gifts, and see myself through Your eyes. Let my life reflect the beauty of Your design. In Jesus' name, Amen."

Reflection Questions

1. In what areas of your life have you believed the lie that you're "*not enough*"?

2. How can you begin to celebrate the unique qualities God has given you, instead of comparing yourself to others?

3. What specific gifts or abilities has God placed in your life that you can use to fulfill His purpose?

Day 7: Co-Heirs with Christ

Memory verse

> "And if children, then heirs—heirs of God and fellow heirs with Christ, provided we suffer with him in order that we may also be glorified with him."
>
> Romans 8:17 (ESV)

Inheritance. It's something most people think about in terms of family wealth or assets being passed down. But the Bible takes the concept of inheritance to a whole new level. If you're a believer, you've inherited something far more valuable than money or possessions—you've inherited the Kingdom of God itself. As co-heirs with Christ, everything that belongs to Him now belongs to us. This isn't just a spiritual slogan—it's a reality that changes how we see ourselves and our future.

The concept of being a co-heir with Christ redefines how we view our worth and position in God's Kingdom. This isn't a hand-me-down inheritance or something earned through performance; it's a gift sealed by Jesus' sacrifice and resurrection. You are not waiting in line for your portion—you've already been given full access to what Christ has secured.

> **Understanding this truth shifts us from living as spiritual beggars to walking as Kingdom heirs, empowered by God's promises and purpose.**

It's easy to think of inheritance as something that's reserved for the future—something we'll experience when we get to heaven. But Scripture makes it clear that our inheritance isn't just a *"someday"* reality. It's a *"right now"* calling. The Kingdom of God isn't just a future destination; it's a present invitation to live in the fullness of Christ's victory. This perspective changes everything. Instead of merely enduring life, we begin to reign in life through Christ, knowing that His power and provision are available to us today.

You Are a Co-Heir with Christ

To be an heir is to have a legal right to something. It means you've been given a share in something valuable, even if you didn't work to earn it. As believers, we are co-heirs with Christ, meaning we share in His inheritance—His Kingdom, His authority, and even His glory. The idea is mind-blowing. Jesus, the King of Kings, shares His inheritance with us, not because of anything we've done, but because of who He is.

> Here's the key: being a co-heir with Christ isn't just about what we receive in the future—it's also about what we have access to right now.

As His co-heirs, we have access to the promises, authority, and power of God here on earth. We're not just waiting for heaven to enjoy the fullness of our inheritance. The Kingdom of God is at hand, and we are called to walk in the authority that comes with being co-heirs with Christ.

However, this identity also comes with a calling. Romans 8:17 reminds us that being co-heirs means sharing in Christ's sufferings as well as His glory. The inheritance isn't just about the reward; it's about walking the same path of sacrifice, service, and obedience that Christ walked.

I Don't Deserve This

One of the biggest barriers to walking in our identity as co-heirs with Christ is the feeling that we don't deserve it. And let's be real—we don't. None of us can earn the right to share in Christ's inheritance. But here's the good news: it was never about what you could earn. It's about what Christ has already won for you.

The enemy would love for you to believe that you're too flawed, too sinful, or too unworthy to inherit anything from God. But when Jesus died and rose again, He sealed your inheritance. It's not up for debate. You are a co-heir, not because you deserve it, but because God has made it so. The moment you accepted Christ, you stepped into the inheritance of eternal life, the Kingdom of God, and a relationship with the Father that can never be taken away.

When Jesus died and rose again, He sealed your inheritance. It's not up for debate. You are a co-heir, not because you deserve it, but because God has made it so. The moment you accepted Christ, you stepped into the inheritance of eternal life, the Kingdom of God, and a relationship with the Father that can never be taken away.

Living as a Co-Heir with Christ

Being a co-heir with Christ isn't just about receiving the reward of eternal life—it's about walking in the authority, power, and purpose God has given you right now. You are not just waiting for your inheritance in heaven; you have access to it today. Let's explore how you can live out this incredible identity as co-heirs with Christ.

1. Walk in Your Authority

As a co-heir with Christ, you have access to His authority. You're not walking through life powerless. You've been given the authority to pray, to speak life, and to stand firm in your faith. Your inheritance isn't passive—it's active. When you face challenges, remember that you're not facing them alone. You are backed by the full authority of heaven.

2. Embrace the Journey of Suffering

Being a co-heir doesn't just mean sharing in Christ's glory—it also means sharing in His suffering. There will be trials, challenges, and moments of sacrifice. But the promise of Romans 8:17 is that as we suffer with Him, we will also be glorified with Him. Your struggles are not in vain. Every step of faith, every act of obedience, is part of the inheritance we share with Christ.

3. Live with Eternity in Mind

While we experience parts of our inheritance now, the fullness of it will be revealed in eternity. As co-heirs, we are destined for eternal life with Christ, where every tear will be wiped away and we will share in His glory forever.

> Don't live for temporary gains—live with eternity in your heart.

The reward is greater than anything the world could ever offer.

Prayer

"Lord, thank You for calling me a co-heir with Christ. I confess that I sometimes feel unworthy of this inheritance, but I choose to believe what You've said about me. Help me to walk in the authority and purpose You've given me, even in the face of trials. Let my life reflect the hope of eternity and the power of Your Kingdom. In Jesus' name, Amen."

Reflection Questions

1. Are there areas in your life where you struggle to believe you have the authority Christ has given you?

2. How can you better embrace the call to share in Christ's sufferings, knowing that it leads to sharing in His glory?

3. What would change in your life if you lived with eternity in mind, rather than focusing on temporary gains?

Day 8: Citizens of Heaven

Memory verse

> "But our citizenship is in heaven. And we eagerly await a Savior from there, the Lord Jesus Christ."
>
> Philippians 3:20 (NIV)

Most of us take pride in where we're from. Whether it's our hometown, country, or culture, our citizenship feels like a part of our identity. But while our earthly citizenship might define where we live or the language we speak, it doesn't tell the whole story. As believers, we belong to a different Kingdom—a heavenly one.

> We're not just tourists passing through earth—we're ambassadors of a Kingdom that's eternal.

Our citizenship isn't ultimately tied to this world. It's tied to heaven. And this changes everything, from how we live to what we live for. And that perspective has the power to shift how we approach everything in life.

You Are a Citizen of Heaven

Being a citizen of heaven means that your true home isn't here on earth. While we live, work, and engage in this world, our ultimate loyalty and identity are rooted in heaven. This isn't a poetic metaphor—it's a spiritual reality. Just as earthly citizens have rights, privileges, and responsibilities, so do we as citizens of God's Kingdom.

What does this mean for your everyday life? It means that your values, priorities, and even your sense of purpose are shaped by heaven, not earth. Earthly citizens might focus on success, status, or material gain, but citizens of heaven live for something far greater. We live for eternity, for the glory of God, and for His Kingdom to come.

But being a citizen of heaven doesn't just mean we wait around for the afterlife. No, as Philippians 3:20 tells us, we live in eager anticipation of Jesus' return while actively representing heaven's culture here on earth. Our words, actions, and choices should reflect the values of the Kingdom we belong to.

> When people encounter us, they should get a taste of what heaven is like.

I'm Too Tied to This World

Let's be honest. It's easy to get wrapped up in the things of this world—whether it's chasing success, worrying about our possessions, or feeling defined by our accomplishments. The world constantly tells us to live for the *"here and now,"* but Scripture reminds us that our real home is elsewhere.

The lie that traps us is that this world is all there is. The enemy wants you to believe that your value, security, and purpose are found in earthly things. But when we start living as though this world is all that matters, we miss the bigger picture. You're not just a citizen of this world—you belong to an eternal Kingdom, and nothing here can compare to the inheritance that awaits you in heaven.

This isn't about detaching from life on earth or ignoring our responsibilities. It's about living with a higher purpose in mind.

> You can't live for eternity if you're focused solely on the temporary.

Your heavenly citizenship calls you to set your mind on things above, not just the things of this world.

Living as a Citizen of Heaven

Being a citizen of heaven changes not just how you see the future, but how you live today. You carry the values, authority, and purpose of God's Kingdom with you wherever you go. Let's explore how you can live out your heavenly citizenship in your everyday life.

1. Live with Heaven's Values

Citizens of heaven don't live by the world's standards. This means choosing love over hate, forgiveness over revenge, and service over selfishness. When you live with heaven's values, you're living counter-culturally. You're showing the world that there's a better way to live—a way that reflects God's Kingdom.

2. Set Your Mind on Eternity

It's easy to get caught up in the day-to-day grind, but citizens of heaven are called to live with eternity in mind. This doesn't mean neglecting your responsibilities; it means holding them in light of what truly lasts. When you focus on the eternal, the temporary worries of this world lose their grip. Keep your eyes on what matters most—God's Kingdom and His glory.

3. Represent Heaven Here and Now

Your citizenship in heaven isn't just for the future—it's for the present. Every interaction you have is an opportunity to reflect the Kingdom of God. When people see the way you live, they should be able to recognize that you're different—not because you're perfect, but because your priorities and values are shaped by a different Kingdom.

> **You are a walking testimony of heaven's reality.**

Discover Who You Are

Prayer

"Lord, thank You for making me a citizen of heaven. I confess that I sometimes get too focused on the things of this world, but today I choose to live with eternity in mind. Help me to reflect Your Kingdom in my words, actions, and choices. Let my life be a testimony of heaven's reality. In Jesus' name, Amen."

Reflection Questions

1. Are there areas in your life where you feel too attached to this world?

2. How can you begin to live with heaven's values, even in a world that often rejects them?

3. What would it look like for you to set your mind on eternity in your daily decisions?

Day 9: Salt and Light

Memory verse

> "You are the salt of the earth... You are the light of the world. A city set on a hill cannot be hidden."
>
> Matthew 5:13-14 (ESV)

Salt and light. Two simple, everyday things, right? But when Jesus says, *"You are the salt of the earth"* and *"You are the light of the world,"* He isn't just making a casual comment—He's making a statement about who you are. In a world that often feels bland and dark, Jesus calls His followers to bring flavor and illumination. He's not telling you to try harder to be salt and light—He's saying that this is already your identity.

But let's be honest—sometimes we forget this truth. We get caught up in our routines, our struggles, and the noise of life. It's easy to feel like we're just blending in or that our impact doesn't matter. But when Jesus called you salt and light, He wasn't speaking hypothetically—He meant it. So the question is: how are you living out that identity today?

You Are the Salt of the Earth and the Light of the World

Let's start with salt. Salt has one main purpose: to enhance flavor. It's a small thing, but without it, food loses its taste. As a believer, you bring flavor to the world—you enhance the lives of those around you by carrying the presence of God. Your influence, no matter how small it seems, has the power to bring life and hope to those who are

Discover Who You Are

spiritually hungry. Just like salt, you make a difference by simply being who God has called you to be.

Then there's light. Light doesn't struggle to be seen. Its very nature is to shine and drive away darkness. Jesus didn't say, *"Try to be the light of the world."* He said, *"You are the light."* Wherever you go, you carry the light of Christ within you. The darkness around you might be overwhelming, but it can never overcome the light you carry.

> **When you walk into a room, you bring the presence of the One who is the light of the world.**

But being salt and light isn't just about passive influence. It's about being intentional in how you live. Salt must be applied to be effective, and light must be uncovered to shine. You are called to actively live out your identity by impacting those around you for the Kingdom. You're not meant to blend in—you're meant to stand out.

I Don't Think I Make a Difference

Maybe you've felt like your life doesn't make much of an impact. The enemy loves to plant seeds of doubt, making you believe that what you do is insignificant. *"What difference can you make?"* he whispers. But here's the truth: God placed you where you are for a reason. He has a purpose for your life, and no act of obedience, no word of encouragement, no prayer goes unnoticed in the Kingdom.

It's easy to look at the overwhelming needs of the world and feel like your light is too small. But remember this:

> light doesn't have to be big to make a difference—it just has to shine.

The impact of your life might not always be visible immediately, but God sees, and He is using you to bring His flavor and His light to those around you. Don't underestimate the power of your influence when it's surrendered to Him.

Living as Salt and Light

Being salt and light isn't just about knowing your identity—it's about living it out daily. You have the power to influence and change the world around you, not by being something you're not, but by being exactly who God has called you to be. Let's explore how you can actively live as the salt and light in a world that desperately needs both.

1. Add Flavor by Your Presence

Salt's value is in its ability to enhance. In the same way, you bring spiritual flavor to every situation you enter. Whether it's in your home, your workplace, or your community, you have the ability to bring life and hope where there was none. Your presence, filled with the Spirit of God, makes a difference. Look for opportunities to encourage, bless, and serve others with the unique flavor God has given you.

2. Shine Intentionally

Light doesn't hide—it shines. As believers, we're called to be visible, not just in word but in action. This doesn't mean you have to be perfect or have all the answers. It means living authentically and reflecting Christ in how you treat others. Let your light shine in your words, your kindness, and your boldness. People should notice something different in how you live.

3. Be a Beacon of Hope

Light serves a purpose—it guides people through darkness. As the light of the world, you have the responsibility of pointing people

> You may be the only source of hope someone encounters today.

toward hope. In a world filled with confusion, pain, and darkness, your life can be a beacon that helps others find their way to Christ.

Shine brightly by living in a way that reflects God's truth and leads others to Him.

Discover Who You Are

Prayer

"Lord, thank You for calling me salt and light. I confess that I sometimes doubt my ability to make a difference, but today I choose to believe that You are using me to bring Your flavor and Your light to the world. Help me to live with intentionality, knowing that even small acts of faithfulness can have a big impact. Let my life reflect Your love and truth in everything I do. In Jesus' name, Amen."

Reflection Questions

1. In what areas of your life have you felt like you're not making a difference?

2. How can you intentionally "*add flavor*" to the lives of those around you this week?

3. What would it look like for you to let your light shine more boldly in your relationships and community?

Day 10: Temple of the Holy Spirit

Memory verse

> "Do you not know that your bodies are temples of the Holy Spirit, who is in you, whom you have received from God? You are not your own; you were bought at a price. Therefore honor God with your bodies."
>
> 1 Corinthians 6:19-20 (NIV)

In a world that's hyper-focused on physical appearance, it's easy to view our bodies through the lens of criticism. We can be hard on ourselves, constantly thinking about what needs improvement. But when God looks at you, He doesn't see just a physical body—He sees a temple. Not an ordinary building, but a sacred place where His Spirit dwells. That changes everything.

What if we started to see our bodies as more than just a vessel we live in? What if we recognized them as the very place where God's Spirit resides? That's exactly what Scripture tells us: Your body is a temple of the Holy Spirit. This isn't just a metaphor—it's your spiritual reality. You carry the presence of God with you wherever you go.

You Are a Temple of the Holy Spirit

The word "*temple*" in Scripture was no casual term. The temple was where God's presence lived among His people. It was a sacred, holy place that required reverence and honor. Now, through Christ, that temple is no longer a physical building—it's you. God has chosen to make His home in you through His Holy Spirit.

Discover Who You Are

Think about what this means: everywhere you go, the Holy Spirit goes. Every decision you make, every word you speak, every action

> **You are a walking sanctuary, carrying the divine presence of God.**

you take is done in the presence of God. This is not meant to weigh you down with guilt or fear but to elevate your understanding of who you are.

That's an incredible privilege and responsibility.

But this isn't just about what we do with our bodies—it's about how we see ourselves. Many of us have a distorted view of our worth, but the fact that God has made His dwelling in us tells us that we are valuable beyond measure. You are not your own—you belong to God. And that truth should shape how you live, how you treat yourself, and how you walk through life.

I Don't Feel Worthy

Let's be honest: it's hard to feel worthy of being called God's temple. We know our flaws, our weaknesses, and the areas where we fall short. How could someone like me be a temple for the Holy Spirit?

But here's the beauty of grace:

> **God doesn't dwell in you because you're perfect; He dwells in you because you're His.**

He chose you. And while we're called to honor God with our bodies, He knows we won't get it right all the time. That's why He gave us the Holy Spirit to help us, guide us, and empower us. You don't have to earn the presence of God—it's His gift to you.

The enemy will try to make you feel disqualified, whispering that you're not good enough to carry God's presence. But remember: God isn't looking for perfection—He's looking for surrender.

> **It's not about being flawless; it's about being faithful.**

Let His Spirit guide you in every part of your life, knowing that He's not leaving anytime soon.

Living as the Temple of the Holy Spirit

Being a temple of the Holy Spirit isn't just a spiritual truth—it's a call to live differently. Your body and your life are sacred because God's Spirit dwells in you. Let's dive deeper into how you can honor God and carry His presence daily

1. Honor God with Your Body

Your body isn't just a physical shell—it's a temple where the Holy Spirit resides. This means treating your body with care, not out of vanity, but out of reverence for the God who dwells within you. Take care of the temple by making choices that honor God. Whether it's through healthy habits, rest, or avoiding things that harm you, honor the One who lives inside you.

2. Invite the Holy Spirit Into Every Area of Your Life

Being a temple means that God is with you in every part of your life—not just the spiritual moments. He wants to be present in your decisions, your relationships, your work, and your struggles. Invite the Holy Spirit into your everyday life, not just when things are difficult. Make space for His voice, and trust that He's guiding you.

3. Carry God's Presence Wherever You Go

As a believer, you carry the Holy Spirit's presence with you into every environment. You don't leave God at church—He's with you at the grocery store, in your workplace, and at home. Be mindful that your actions and words reflect the God who lives inside you. You are a walking testimony of His presence.

Prayer

"Lord, thank You for making my body a temple of Your Holy Spirit. I confess that I don't always live in a way that reflects this truth, but today I choose to honor You with my body and my life. Help me to invite Your presence into every area and live in a way that glorifies You. Let my life be a reflection of Your holiness and grace. In Jesus' name, Amen."

Reflection Questions

1. How does knowing you are the temple of the Holy Spirit change the way you see yourself?

2. Are there areas of your life where you need to invite the Holy Spirit's presence more intentionally?

3. What steps can you take to better honor God with your body and your actions?

Day 11: Set Free in Christ

Memory verse

> "It is for freedom that Christ has set us free. Stand firm, then, and do not let yourselves be burdened again by a yoke of slavery."
>
> *Galatians 5:1 (NIV)*

Freedom. It's something people fight for, sing about, and dream of. But if we're honest, many of us still live with invisible chains—fear, guilt, shame, or addiction. The world offers freedom in so many ways, but most of it is temporary, and some of it is counterfeit. Real freedom—the kind that transforms lives—only comes through Christ.

> **Jesus didn't just come to make you feel better—He came to set you free.**

But here's the challenge: even after being set free, many of us still live as though we're in chains. We've been released from the bondage of sin, but sometimes we go back to what's familiar, even if it's harmful. The good news is that when Christ sets you free, you're free indeed.

> **But to live in that freedom, you have to stop going back to the things that once held you captive.**

You Are Set Free in Christ

Freedom isn't just a nice idea; it's your reality in Christ. When Jesus died and rose again, He broke the power of sin and death over your life. This means that whatever once held you captive—whether it was fear, addiction, guilt, or shame—has lost its grip on you. You're no longer a prisoner—you're free.

But freedom in Christ is more than just escaping the chains of sin. It's the freedom to live fully, to walk in purpose, and to experience the abundant life that Jesus promised. Galatians 5:1 reminds us that Christ set us free for the sake of freedom itself. He didn't set you free just so you could survive—He set you free so you could thrive.

Still, we have to make the choice to walk in that freedom daily. It's possible to be free and yet live like we're still bound. Old habits, lies from the enemy, and even our own insecurities can try to pull us back into slavery. But the truth is that you've been given everything you need to live in freedom—you just have to stand firm and refuse to let those old chains define you.

I Feel Stuck in My Struggles

Even as believers, we sometimes feel stuck. We know we've been set free, but it feels like we're still trapped in the same old patterns, whether it's anxiety, sin, or insecurity. The enemy's tactic is to convince you that your freedom isn't real, that you're still a slave to whatever held you down before.

But here's the truth: Your feelings don't define your freedom—Christ does. The power of sin and fear was broken the moment you placed your faith in Jesus. The chains are gone, and the prison door is open. It's time to stop living like you're still in bondage and start walking in the freedom that's already yours. Don't let old lies convince you that you're still stuck.

Freedom in Christ isn't a feeling—it's a fact. And even if you don't always feel free, you can choose to live in that truth. Freedom begins with believing what Jesus has already done for you.

Living in the Freedom of Christ

Being set free in Christ is more than just a momentary experience—it's a lifestyle. It's about choosing to live in the freedom that Jesus has already purchased for you. Let's look at how you can walk in that freedom daily and refuse to go back to the things that once held you captive.

1. Refuse to Go Back

Just because you've been set free doesn't mean the temptation to go back to old ways will disappear. The enemy will try to lure you back into the same patterns of sin or fear that once enslaved you. But Galatians 5:1 urges you to *"stand firm"* in your freedom. Refuse to go back to the things that once held you captive. When you feel the pull to return to old habits, remind yourself that those chains have been broken.

2. Renew Your Mind with Truth

Living in freedom requires more than just trying harder—it requires renewing your mind with the truth of God's Word.

> **What you believe shapes how you live.**

If you believe you're still bound, you'll live like it. But if you believe that Christ has set you free, you'll start to experience that freedom in every part of your life. Spend time in Scripture, reminding yourself of who you are in Christ and the freedom He has given you.

3. Walk in the Power of the Holy Spirit

Freedom doesn't come from your own strength—it comes from the power of the Holy Spirit working in you. He's the one who enables you to break free from old patterns and walk in new life. The Holy Spirit is your guide and your source of strength. When you feel weak, lean into His power. Let Him remind you of the freedom that's already yours in Christ.

Prayer

"Lord, thank You for setting me free. I confess that I sometimes feel stuck in old patterns or struggles, but today I choose to believe that Your freedom is real. Help me to stand firm in that freedom and to refuse the lies that try to pull me back. Let Your Holy Spirit guide me and empower me to live the abundant life You have promised. In Jesus' name, Amen."

Reflection Questions

1. What are the old habits or lies that try to pull you back into bondage?

2. How can you stand firm in the freedom Christ has given you?

3. What role does the Holy Spirit play in helping you live out your freedom in Christ?

Day 12: Branches of the True Vine

Memory verse

> "I am the vine; you are the branches. If you remain in me and I in you, you will bear much fruit; apart from me you can do nothing."
>
> John 15:5 (NIV)

We live in a culture that celebrates independence—doing things on our own, making our own way, and proving that we don't need help. But when Jesus describes our identity, He doesn't celebrate independence; He emphasizes connection. In John 15:5, Jesus reminds us that we are branches connected to Him, the true vine. The branch has no life of its own apart from the vine, and that's the point: our identity is tied directly to our relationship with Him.

The world says, *"Do it yourself."* Jesus says, *"Remain in me."* The two couldn't be more different. So who do you think you are—someone who has to make it on your own, or someone connected to the source of life itself?

You Are a Branch of the True Vine

To be a branch of the true vine means that you are intimately connected to Jesus. You aren't a disconnected bystander; you are part of His life-giving source. Just as a branch draws its nutrients and strength from the vine, you draw everything you need from your relationship with Christ.

This connection isn't a one-time event; it's ongoing. Jesus tells us to remain in Him, meaning we are to stay close, stay dependent, and stay connected.

Identity Revolution

> **The life you desire, the fruit you want to bear, all come from being rooted in Him.**

A branch that isn't connected to the vine withers and dies because it has no source of life on its own. The same is true for us spiritually.

But when you remain in Christ, the true vine, you not only survive—you thrive. You produce fruit, not through your own strength but through His. The more connected you are to Him, the more your life reflects His character, love, and power. The vine supplies everything the branch needs to grow and flourish. You are not self-sufficient, but you are fully supplied.

I Feel Disconnected

Maybe there are seasons where you've felt spiritually dry—like you're just going through the motions or that the connection between you and God feels distant. The truth is, we all have moments like that. But here's what you need to remember: Jesus is always the vine, and He never disconnects from you. If you feel disconnected, the invitation is simple—remain in Him.

Remaining in Christ isn't about striving or trying harder; it's about surrendering and drawing close to the One who sustains you. The enemy loves to make you feel like you're cut off or that you have to figure it out on your own, but that's a lie. The vine hasn't left you. Jesus is always there, ready to provide the life, strength, and nourishment you need.

The question is, are you remaining in Him? Are you seeking His presence daily, depending on Him for everything, and trusting that apart from Him, you can do nothing?

Living as a Branch of the True Vine

Being a branch of the true vine is an ongoing relationship. It's about staying connected to Jesus, drawing life from Him, and trusting in His provision. Let's look at what it means to remain in Christ daily and how this connection leads to a fruitful life.

1. Stay Connected Through Prayer and the Word

A branch doesn't survive apart from the vine, and in the same way, we can't thrive spiritually without remaining connected to Christ through prayer and His Word. Daily connection is your lifeline. Make it a priority to spend time with God, not out of obligation but out of the desire to stay close to the One who sustains you.

2. Trust in God's Supply

The vine provides everything the branch needs to grow and bear fruit. If you're feeling weary or like you're striving to make things happen on your own, it's time to trust in God's supply. He's already given you everything you need in Christ. Instead of relying on your own strength, lean into His provision.

3. Bear Fruit That Lasts

Fruitfulness isn't measured by worldly success; it's measured by the character and impact that comes from abiding in Christ. The fruit of the Spirit—love, joy, peace, patience—comes from a life rooted in Him. When you remain in Jesus, the fruit you bear will reflect His heart and His Kingdom. It won't fade or wither, because it's sustained by the true vine.

Discover Who You Are

Prayer

"Lord, thank You for being the true vine that sustains me. I confess that there are times I try to do things on my own or feel disconnected from You, but today I choose to remain in You. Help me to stay connected to You through prayer and Your Word, and let my life bear fruit that reflects Your character. Thank You for always providing everything I need. In Jesus' name, Amen."

Reflection Questions

1. Are there areas of your life where you feel disconnected from Christ?

2. How can you prioritize remaining in Him through prayer, worship, and the Word?

3. What kind of fruit are you bearing in this season, and how can you stay more connected to the true vine to bear fruit that lasts?

Day 13: Overcomers Through Christ

Memory verse

> "No, in all these things we are more than conquerors through him who loved us."
>
> *Romans 8:37 (NIV)*

Identity Revolution

Life can feel like an endless series of battles. Some days it feels like you're just trying to survive, let alone conquer anything. But here's the thing—God didn't create you just to survive. He made you to overcome. Romans 8:37 doesn't say you're barely making it; it says you're more than a conqueror. That means no matter what you're facing—whether it's a tough season, spiritual warfare, or personal struggles—you're not fighting for victory, you're fighting from victory.

But if we're honest, we don't always feel like overcomers, do we? Sometimes the weight of life feels too heavy, the battles too fierce. Yet, God's Word reminds us that our identity is rooted in what Christ has done, not in what we feel.

Victory isn't a feeling; it's a fact

—and that fact is found in Jesus.

You Are an Overcomer Through Christ

Being an overcomer doesn't mean you'll never face challenges, difficulties, or seasons of struggle. In fact, Jesus Himself said we'd face trouble in this world (John 16:33). But the good news is that our victory has already been secured through His life, death, and resurrection. You are not just scraping by—you are more than a

Discover Who You Are

conqueror because Christ has already conquered sin, death, and every obstacle that stands in your way.

This doesn't mean that every battle will feel easy. There will be moments when you feel weak, defeated, or even on the verge of giving up. But here's where the power of being an overcomer in Christ shines through: your strength doesn't come from you—it comes from Him. When you feel like you've got nothing left, that's when God steps in with His supernatural strength and carries you through.

The battles you face are real, but they are not the end of the story. Christ's victory on the cross has already secured your outcome. You may be in a fight right now, but remember:

> **You are fighting from a place of victory, not for it.**

That makes all the difference.

I Feel Defeated

Sometimes, life leaves us feeling more defeated than victorious. The enemy loves to capitalize on those moments, whispering lies that make us doubt God's promises. *"You'll never overcome this,"* he says. *"You're too weak. This problem is too big."*

But here's the truth: Victory isn't based on how strong you feel—it's based on how strong Christ is. Even when you feel weak, Christ's power is perfected in your weakness (2 Corinthians 12:9). The enemy wants you to believe that your struggles define you, but God says you are defined by His victory. Feeling defeated doesn't change the fact that Christ has already won.

It's easy to focus on the battle right in front of you and forget that the war has already been won. When you feel overwhelmed, remember that the battle belongs to the Lord, and He is fighting for you. You are an overcomer, not because of what you can do, but because of what Christ has done. Don't let temporary setbacks convince you that victory isn't yours.

Living as an Overcomer Through Christ

> Being an overcomer in Christ doesn't mean the battle won't come, but it does mean the outcome has already been decided.

Discover Who You Are

You're not fighting alone or in your own strength. Let's look at how you can stand firm in the truth of your victory and live as the overcomer God has called you to be.

1. Stand on God's Promises

Overcoming isn't about ignoring reality—it's about standing firm in the promises of God, no matter what you see in front of you.

> **God's promises are stronger than your problems.**

When life feels overwhelming, anchor yourself in the truth of Scripture. Remind yourself that God has already declared victory over sin, death, and every challenge you face. His Word never changes, even when your circumstances do.

2. Rely on God's Strength, Not Your Own

One of the greatest truths about being an overcomer is that you don't have to do it in your own strength. God's power works best in your weakness. Instead of trying to muscle through your battles on your own, invite God into your struggle. Let His strength carry you when you're weary, and trust that His power will help you overcome whatever you're facing.

3. Keep an Eternal Perspective

Sometimes we lose sight of the bigger picture. Life's challenges can feel all-consuming, but remember that your identity as an overcomer is rooted in eternity. This life is temporary, but Christ's victory is forever. Keeping an eternal perspective helps you navigate the ups and downs with faith, knowing that your story doesn't end with defeat. In Christ, your future is secure, and ultimate victory is guaranteed.

Prayer

"Lord, thank You for calling me an overcomer through Christ. I confess that there are times I feel defeated and weak, but today I choose to stand in the victory You've already won for me. Help me to rely on Your strength and not my own, and remind me that Your promises are greater than my problems. Let my life reflect the truth that in You, I am more than a conqueror. In Jesus' name, Amen."

Reflection Questions

1. In what areas of your life do you feel more defeated than victorious?

2. How can you rely on God's strength instead of trying to fight your battles on your own?

3. What promises from Scripture can you stand on today to remind yourself that you are more than a conqueror in Christ?

Day 14: Friends of God

Memory verse

> "I no longer call you servants, because a servant does not know his master's business. Instead, I have called you friends, for everything that I learned from my Father I have made known to you."
>
> John 15:15 (NIV)

Most of us grow up thinking of God as distant—someone to be respected, worshiped, and revered. And He is all of that, but what if I told you He's also your friend? Not in a casual, *"Hey, what's up"* kind of way, but in a deep, personal, intimate way that changes everything about how you relate to Him. In John 15:15, Jesus takes the idea of relationship with God to a whole new level when He says, *"I have called you friends."* Imagine that—the Creator of the universe calls you His friend.

But let's be real. How often do we live like we're friends with God? It's easy to slip into thinking of Him as someone who's far off, or like a boss we're trying to impress. But Jesus is clear—this is not a master-servant relationship. It's a friendship built on love, trust, and shared purpose.

You Are a Friend of God

To be called a friend of God is one of the most amazing truths of our identity in Christ. In Jesus' time, servants were expected to obey without question—they didn't have access to the plans or intimate thoughts of their masters. But Jesus shifts the relationship. You are no longer just a servant—you are His friend. And that means you're invited into His plans, His heart, and His presence in a way that's deeply personal.

Discover Who You Are

Friendship with God isn't something you have to earn. It's something Jesus offers freely. He didn't just make you His servant or follower—He brought you into a friendship where you can walk closely with Him. And just like any good friendship, it's built on trust, communication, and shared experience.

> **God doesn't just want your service—He wants your friendship.**

But here's where it gets even better: as God's friend, you're not on the outside looking in. Jesus said, *"Everything I learned from my Father I have made known to you."* In other words, God has brought you into His inner circle. You're not in the dark about His plans. He shares His heart with you because He trusts you, loves you, and wants to be close to you.

I Don't Feel Close to God

> **You're not a distant follower—you're a trusted friend.**

It's one thing to know God calls you His friend, but it's another to feel that closeness in your daily life. Maybe you've felt distant from

God, or like He's more of an authority figure than a friend. It's easy to fall into the mindset that we need to earn God's approval before we can approach Him. But friendship with God isn't based on how well you perform—it's based on His love for you.

If you've ever felt disconnected or distant, remember this:

> **God never withdraws His friendship.**

He is always inviting you to draw closer. Sometimes life's distractions, fears, or even our own mistakes can make us feel far away from Him, but God hasn't moved. He's still your friend, waiting to walk with you through whatever you're facing. His friendship is steady, unchanging, and full of grace.

Living as a Friend of God

Being a friend of God isn't just a comforting idea, it's a relationship that changes how we live, how we pray, and how we handle life's challenges. Let's explore what it looks like to live as God's friend, not just in moments of need, but in every aspect of our daily walk.

1. Cultivate Your Friendship Through Prayer

Just like with any friendship, communication is key. Prayer isn't just a ritual; it's a conversation with your closest friend.

> **Spend time talking to God as you would with someone you trust.**

Share your heart, your struggles, and your joys with Him. He wants to hear from you, not just in formal moments, but throughout your day.

2. Listen for God's Voice

Friendship with God isn't just about talking—it's about listening, too. Jesus said He shares everything with His friends. This means God has things He wants to share with you. Make space to listen to His voice, whether it's through His Word, prayer, or moments of stillness. A true friend listens, and God is ready to speak into your life if you take time to hear Him.

3. Trust in God's Friendship During Trials

True friends stick with you through hard times. When life gets tough, it's easy to feel like God is distant or silent, but remember—

He's your friend. He's walking with you through the valley, even when you can't see it. Trust in His presence and His promises, knowing that His friendship never wavers, even when life is difficult.

Prayer

"Lord, thank You for calling me Your friend. I confess that there are times I feel distant or like I need to earn Your approval, but today I choose to believe in the closeness of our friendship. Help me to cultivate this relationship through prayer and trust, and remind me that You are always with me, even in hard times. Let my life reflect the deep friendship we share. In Jesus' name, Amen."

Reflection Questions

1. How does knowing you are a friend of God change the way you approach Him in prayer?

2. Are there areas of your life where you feel distant from God? How can you begin to cultivate deeper friendship with Him?

3. What would change in your life if you trusted God as a close friend, even in the midst of trials?

Day 15: Loved by God

Memory verse

"For I am convinced that neither death nor life, neither angels nor demons, neither the present nor the future, nor any powers, neither height nor depth, nor anything else in all creation, will be able to separate us from the love of God that is in Christ Jesus our Lord."

Romans 8:38-39 (NIV)

We live in a world that often ties love to performance—how well you behave, what you achieve, or how you measure up to others' expectations. But God's love doesn't work like that.

> **His love is not based on what you do but on who He is.**

You are deeply and unconditionally loved by God, and nothing can change that.

For many of us, this idea is hard to grasp. We're so used to love being conditional—based on how well we perform or how much we deserve it—that it can feel strange to be loved without strings attached. But that's the reality of God's love: it is unshakable, even in your worst moments.

God's love doesn't wait for you to clean up your mess; it meets you in the middle of it. It's the kind of love that steps into our brokenness and says, *"You are still mine,"* even when we feel unworthy or unlovable.

You Are Loved by God

The love of God isn't just a concept or a comforting thought—it's the foundation of who you are. Before you were born, before you made any mistakes, and before you even knew Him, God loved you. He chose you, not because you earned it, but because that's who He is.

Romans 8:38-39 paints a powerful picture of how inseparable God's love is. Nothing—literally nothing—can separate you from His love. No sin is too great, no failure too large, and no circumstance too overwhelming to change how God feels about you. His love is constant, unwavering, and complete. And because His love isn't based on what you do, it doesn't change when you fall short.

But here's where it gets even better: God doesn't just love you in a distant or abstract way. He loves you personally, intimately, and specifically. You are not overlooked by God—you are loved by Him right where you are, flaws and all. That love defines you and anchors you through every season of life.

But Does God Still Love ME?

It's easy to feel like God's love is for someone else—someone who has it all together, who hasn't made the same mistakes, or who seems more "*worthy*." But here's the truth:

> **God's love was never about your worthiness; it's about His grace.**

The enemy loves to make you feel like you're too broken, too flawed, or too far gone to be loved by God. But Scripture is clear—nothing can separate you from His love.

In fact, it's precisely in those moments of brokenness that God's love shines the brightest. God doesn't wait for you to become 'enough'—He steps into your story exactly where you are. His love isn't diminished by your mistakes or overshadowed by your failures. Instead, it surrounds you in your darkest moments, offering hope and healing that only He can provide.

When you feel unworthy, remind yourself that God's love isn't earned. You can't perform your way into His love or fail your way out of it. You are already fully loved by Him. Whether you feel it or not, His love is as real and constant as the air you breathe.

Living as Someone Loved by God

Being loved by God is not just a comforting truth, but part of your identity that changes everything. You are fully, deeply, and unconditionally loved, and that love is meant to shape how you live, how you relate to others, and how you see yourself. Let's explore how you can live in the reity of God's love every day.

1. Receive God's Love Daily

God's love isn't something you just know in your head—it's something you can experience daily.

> Take time each day to remind yourself of His love for you.

Spend time in prayer, letting His love fill the places where you feel empty or unworthy. Receiving God's love is the first step to living in the fullness of who you are.

2. Live from Love, Not for Love

The world teaches us to perform for approval, but as believers, we're called to live from a place of love, not striving for it. Let God's love be the foundation of everything you do. When you live from a place of being fully loved, your actions flow from security and freedom, not from the pressure to earn approval.

3. Share God's Love with Others

The love you've received from God isn't just for you—it's meant to be shared. As you experience His love, let it overflow into your relationships. When you love others, you reflect God's heart to the world around you. Whether through acts of kindness, words of encouragement, or simply being present, let God's love flow through you.

Discover Who You Are

Prayer

"Lord, thank You for loving me unconditionally. I confess that I sometimes feel unworthy or distant from Your love, but today I choose to believe that nothing can separate me from it. Help me to live in the reality of Your love every day, and let it overflow into the way I treat others. Thank You for loving me completely, just as I am. In Jesus' name, Amen."

Reflection Questions

1. Are there areas in your life where you struggle to feel worthy of God's love?

2. How can you remind yourself daily that you are loved by God, even in your imperfect moments?

3. How can you share the love of God with those around you this week?

Day 16: Forgiven

Memory Verse

> "If we confess our sins, he is faithful and just and will forgive us our sins and purify us from all unrighteousness."
>
> 1 John 1:9 (NIV)

We've all made mistakes. Whether it's something small or something we deeply regret, the weight of guilt can feel overwhelming at times. But here's the good news: you are forgiven. Your mistakes, sins, and failures don't define you—God's grace does. In Christ, you are not just pardoned, but completely forgiven, washed clean, and made new.

Forgiveness isn't just something God gives; it's a part of your identity. You are forgiven, not because of anything you did, but because of what Christ did for you. And that forgiveness doesn't run out—it's permanent, unshakable, and complete.

Think about that for a moment: the Creator of the universe, the One who knows every detail of your life, looks at you and says, *"You are forgiven."* He doesn't hold your past mistakes over you or remind you of your failures. Instead, He offers a clean slate, inviting you into a new beginning. This kind of forgiveness isn't just a second chance; it's an invitation to live free from the chains of guilt and shame.

Forgiveness is more than just wiping away sin—it's about restoration. God doesn't just forgive you; He redeems you, restoring what was broken and calling you into a life of purpose and peace. To be forgiven isn't just to be free from the past; it's to be empowered for the future. His grace doesn't just erase—it transforms, giving you the strength to walk forward in the fullness of His love.

You Are Forgiven

Being forgiven means that your past no longer has the power to condemn you. Jesus paid the price for your sins on the cross, and because of that, your slate has been wiped clean.

> **You are not defined by your worst moments, but by God's mercy.**

His forgiveness isn't conditional, based on how well you perform—it's rooted in His love for you.

1 John 1:9 tells us that if we confess our sins, God is faithful and just to forgive us. And He doesn't just forgive; He cleanses us from all unrighteousness.

> **You don't have to carry the weight of guilt or shame anymore.**

Jesus has already carried that burden for you. You are forgiven, and that forgiveness is the foundation for living a life of freedom and purpose.

This identity as *"forgiven"* gives you the freedom to move forward without the chains of the past holding you back.

> **You don't have to live in the shadow of your mistakes.**

Instead, you can live in the light of God's grace, knowing that His forgiveness has covered everything.

I Struggle to Accept Forgiveness

For many of us, accepting God's forgiveness can be difficult. We believe He's forgiven us, but we still feel the weight of guilt or shame. It's easy to think that our sin is too great or that we've messed up too many times. But here's the truth: God's forgiveness isn't limited by your past—it's defined by His love.

The enemy loves to remind us of our failures, whispering that we're not truly forgiven. But those are lies. When Jesus said, *"It is finished,"* He meant it. Your sins have been paid for in full. There's nothing left for you to earn or prove. You don't have to keep punishing yourself for something that God has already forgiven.

Forgiveness doesn't depend on how you feel—it depends on God's promise.

> **If God says you're forgiven, then you are forgiven, period.**

Living as Someone Forgiven

Being forgiven changes everything. It frees you from the weight of the past and gives you the confidence to live in the fullness of God's grace. Let's explore how you can live as someone who is fully forgiven and walk in the freedom that comes with that identity.

1. Let Go of Guilt

Guilt has a way of clinging to us, even when we know we're forgiven. But God calls you to live in freedom, not in guilt.

> **Let go of the weight that Jesus already took from you.**

When those feelings of guilt rise up, remind yourself of the truth: you are forgiven, completely and fully.

2. Forgive Yourself

Sometimes the hardest person to forgive is yourself. Even though God has forgiven you, you might still hold on to regret or shame. But if God, in His perfect holiness, has forgiven you, who are you to hold on to what He has already released? Give yourself the grace that God has already extended to you.

3. Live in the Freedom of Forgiveness

Forgiveness isn't just about being released from the past—it's about stepping into the freedom of a new life. God's forgiveness sets you free to live without the chains of regret, allowing you to walk in joy, peace, and purpose. Let His grace propel you forward, unburdened by the past.

Prayer

"Lord, thank You for the gift of forgiveness. I confess that I sometimes struggle to accept that I am fully forgiven, but today I choose to believe Your promise. Help me to let go of guilt and shame, and teach me to walk in the freedom of Your grace. Thank You for wiping my slate clean and giving me a fresh start. In Jesus' name, Amen."

Reflection Questions

1. Are there areas of your life where you still struggle to accept God's forgiveness?

2. How can you let go of guilt and live in the freedom that forgiveness brings?

3. What steps can you take to extend grace and forgiveness to yourself, as God has already forgiven you?

Day 17: Holy and Blameless

Memory Verse

"For he chose us in him before the creation of the world to be holy and blameless in his sight."

Ephesians 1:4 (NIV)

When you hear the words *"holy"* and *"blameless,"* what comes to mind? For many, it sounds like an impossible standard—something only a select few can achieve. But in Christ, holiness and blamelessness are not things you have to earn; they are part of your identity. God chose you before the creation of the world to be set apart and to live in freedom from guilt and shame. You are already declared holy and blameless because of what Jesus has done for you.

This isn't just a future promise—it's a present reality. Holiness and blamelessness aren't reserved for some far-off moment in eternity; they are truths you can walk in today. When God chose you, He didn't do it halfway. He called you into a life free from condemnation, marked by His grace and the righteousness of Christ.

> **Holiness isn't a status you earn; it's a gift you've already received.**

And this gift transforms everything. It shifts your focus from striving for perfection to resting in God's finished work. It replaces the shame of your past with the security of knowing you are loved and accepted.

> Holiness and blamelessness aren't just about how God sees you—they're about how His grace empowers you to live.

In Christ, your identity is no longer defined by your failures, but by His faithfulness.

You Are Holy and Blameless

Being holy means being set apart for God's purposes, and being blameless means that through Christ, you are free from guilt. It's easy to think that holiness and blamelessness are based on our behavior, but that's not the case. God sees you as holy and blameless because of Christ's sacrifice. When Jesus died for your sins, He didn't just cover them—He removed them, making you pure in God's eyes.

Ephesians 1:4 tells us that God chose us to be holy and blameless in His sight. This isn't something you have to strive for; it's a truth you can live in. You don't have to carry the weight of your past mistakes because God has already declared you righteous through Jesus. Your holiness and blamelessness aren't dependent on your perfection—they're rooted in God's grace.

This means that when God looks at you, He sees you through the lens of Christ's righteousness. You are no longer defined by your failures or shortcomings—you are defined by God's declaration that you are holy, pure, and spotless.

I Don't Feel Holy or Blameless

Maybe you've struggled to believe that you could ever be holy or blameless. You might feel weighed down by past sins, current struggles, or the feeling that you're constantly falling short. But here's the truth:

> **God's view of you isn't based on your feelings—it's based on Christ's finished work.**

You may feel unworthy, but in Christ, you are already declared holy and blameless.

Feelings can be powerful, but they aren't always truthful. When guilt or shame creeps in, it's easy to mistake those emotions for reality. But God's Word is the ultimate truth, and His declaration of who you are carries far more weight than your momentary feelings. Your worth isn't determined by your perception of yourself but by God's declaration over you. Trusting this truth allows you to rise above the accusations of the enemy and live in the confidence of who God says you are.

The enemy loves to remind us of our mistakes, whispering that we'll never measure up. But your identity isn't about measuring up; it's about what Christ has already done. You are covered by His righteousness, and nothing can change that. When you feel less than holy, remind yourself that God sees you through the lens of grace.

Living as Holy and Blameless

Living as someone who is holy and blameless is not about trying harder or being perfect. It's about embracing the truth of who you already are in Christ. You are set apart, forgiven, and free to live without guilt or shame. Let's explore how you can walk confidently in your identity as someone who is holy and blameless.

1. Walk in Confidence, Not Condemnation

It's easy to let guilt or shame hold you back, but God has called you to walk in confidence. You don't have to live under the weight of condemnation. Romans 8:1 reminds us that there is no condemnation for those who are in Christ. Because you are holy and blameless in His sight, you can live with freedom and boldness, knowing that you are fully accepted by God.

2. Reflect God's Holiness in Your Life

Holiness isn't just about being set apart—it's about living in a way that reflects God's character. As someone who is already declared holy, you are called to live in a way that reflects who God is. Let your actions, your words, and your decisions be shaped by the holiness that God has placed within you. You're not striving for holiness—you're living out the holiness that is already yours.

3. Remember You Are Free from Blame

Blamelessness means that God no longer holds your sins against you.

> You don't have to live in fear of punishment or rejection.

Christ's sacrifice has washed you clean, and you are free to live without the burden of past mistakes. When guilt tries to creep in, stand firm in the truth that you are blameless before God because of what Jesus has done.

Discover Who You Are

Prayer

"Lord, thank You for choosing me to be holy and blameless in Your sight. I confess that there are times I feel unworthy or weighed down by guilt, but today I choose to believe Your Word. Help me to walk confidently in the truth that I am set apart and forgiven. Let my life reflect Your holiness, and remind me daily that I am free from all blame. In Jesus' name, Amen."

Reflection Questions

1. Are there areas of your life where you struggle to believe you are truly holy and blameless?

2. How can you remind yourself daily of the truth that God sees you through the lens of Christ's righteousness?

3. What would change in your life if you embraced your identity as someone who is fully forgiven and free from guilt?

Day 18: Part of the Body of Christ

Memory verse

> "Now you are the body of Christ, and each one of you is a part of it."
>
> 1 Corinthians 12:27 (NIV)

It's easy to feel like we're just one small person in a big world—like our individual efforts don't really make a difference. But in Christ, you are part of something far bigger than yourself. You are part of the body of Christ, and that means you have a unique role to play. Each member of the body is essential, and God has designed you with specific gifts, abilities, and purposes to contribute to the whole.

This isn't just about finding a place to belong; it's about recognizing your God-given purpose within His Kingdom.

> **You were not saved to sit on the sidelines—you were saved to step into the game.**

Your life, experiences, and talents are intentional, woven into God's plan to build His church and reach the world. Whether you see it or not, your role carries eternal significance because it contributes to something far greater than any one of us.

When we look at the church as a whole, it can feel overwhelming. How do my small actions fit into such a massive, global movement? But God's Word assures us that every single member of the body matters. You are not overlooked by God; you are chosen by Him for a purpose only you can fulfill. You are not just a number in the crowd or a face in the pew. You are a vital piece of the puzzle, a thread in the tapestry of God's redemptive story.

You're not on the sidelines. You're an integral part of God's plan for His church and His Kingdom.

Your role matters—not because of its size, but because of the One who called you to it. When we embrace this truth, it changes how we see ourselves and how we approach our place in the body of Christ. Together, we form a complete, thriving body, united by one Spirit and one mission.

You Are Part of the Body of Christ

In 1 Corinthians 12, Paul uses the analogy of a human body to describe the church, calling believers the body of Christ. Each part of the body has a specific function, and every part is necessary for the whole body to function properly. You are one of those essential parts. Your gifts, talents, and experiences are not random—they are purposefully given by God to help build up His church and advance His Kingdom.

It can be tempting to think that some roles are more important than others, but Paul makes it clear that every part of the body is vital. The hand can't say to the eye, "*I don't need you,*" and the eye can't say to the foot, "*I don't need you.*" Just as each part of the human body serves a unique purpose, your role in the body of Christ is crucial. You have been specifically placed in God's family to fulfill a calling that only you can fulfill.

Being part of the body of Christ also means that you are never alone. You belong to a community of believers who support, encourage, and strengthen each other. You are part of something bigger than yourself, and together, we are stronger than we could ever be individually.

I Don't Feel Like I Have Anything to Offer

Maybe you've felt like you don't have much to contribute. You might wonder, *"What do I really bring to the table?"* But here's the truth:

> **God has uniquely gifted you for a reason.**

You have been placed in the body of Christ to play a role that no one else can play. Even if you feel like your gifts are small or insignificant, they are invaluable in God's eyes.

The enemy would love to make you feel like you're unimportant or that your contribution doesn't matter. But the truth is, every part of the body is essential. Whether you're serving in the background or leading up front, God sees your faithfulness and values your role.

Discover Who You Are

You are needed, and your gifts are an important part of what God is doing through His church.

Living as Part of the Body of Christ

Being part of the body of Christ means that you have a unique and important role to play. You are not just an individual—you are part of something bigger. Let's explore how you can embrace your role and contribute to the health and mission of God's Kingdom.

1. *Discover Your Spiritual Gifts*

God has given each of us unique gifts and abilities that are meant to be used for His Kingdom. Take time to discover your spiritual gifts by praying, seeking guidance from others, and reflecting on the things you're passionate about. When you know the gifts God has placed in you, you'll be better equipped to serve with purpose.

2. *Embrace Your Role*

Your role in the body of Christ is unique and irreplaceable. Instead of comparing yourself to others, embrace the role God has given you and the gifts He's placed within you. When you embrace your identity and role in the church, you allow God to use you in ways you might not have imagined.

3. Serve Faithfully

Being part of the body of Christ isn't just about discovering your gifts—it's about using them to serve others. Commit to serving faithfully wherever God has called you. Whether your role is upfront or behind the scenes, your service is valuable, and God will use it to strengthen His church and bless others.

Discover Who You Are

Prayer

"Lord, thank You for making me part of the body of Christ. I confess that I sometimes feel like my role isn't important, but I choose to believe that You have uniquely gifted me for a purpose. Help me to embrace my role and serve faithfully, knowing that I am a vital part of Your Kingdom. Strengthen my connection with other believers, and let my life reflect Your love and grace. In Jesus' name, Amen."

Reflection Questions

1. What gifts or abilities has God given you that can be used to serve the body of Christ?

2. Are there ways you've been hesitant to step into your role within the church or community? What's holding you back?

3. How can you build stronger connections with other believers to support and encourage each other in your roles?

Day 19: Victorious in Christ

Memory verse

> "But thanks be to God! He gives us the victory through our Lord Jesus Christ."
>
> *1 Corinthians 15:57 (NIV)*

Life can feel like a constant battle—whether it's struggles at work, difficulties in relationships, or even inner battles with fear, doubt, or temptation. But here's the good news: you are already victorious in Christ. This victory isn't based on your strength or ability, but on what Jesus has already done. You're not fighting for victory—you're fighting from a place of victory.

The world tells us that victory looks like success, power, or never facing failure. But in Christ, victory looks different. It means overcoming sin, walking in freedom, and trusting that God has already won the ultimate battle.

> You are victorious, not because of what you can do, but because of what Jesus has done for

You Are Victorious in Christ

The victory that Christ won on the cross was final and complete.

> He defeated sin, death, and every power of darkness.

And because of that, you can live in victory, no matter what challenges you face. This victory doesn't mean you'll never face

Discover Who You Are

struggles, but it does mean that those struggles don't define you. Your identity is rooted in the fact that Christ has already won.

1 Corinthians 15:57 reminds us that God has given us the victory through our Lord Jesus Christ. This is not a victory we have to earn or fight for—it's already been given to us. Jesus fought the battle on your behalf, and now you get to live in the freedom and victory that He purchased for you. When you face difficulties, you can stand firm, knowing that the outcome has already been decided—Jesus wins, and because of that, so do you.

This victory isn't just about overcoming external circumstances—it's about conquering the internal battles as well.

> **Fear, doubt, and temptation may come, but they no longer have power over you because Christ's victory is your victory.**

The cross wasn't just a moment in history; it was a declaration for eternity that you are free, loved, and victorious. No matter how overwhelming your struggles may feel, you can walk with confidence, knowing that the same power that raised Christ from the dead is alive and at work in you.

I Feel Like I'm losing

We all go through seasons where we don't feel victorious. Life gets hard, and it can seem like defeat is all around us. Maybe you're going through a struggle right now, and victory feels like a distant dream. But here's the truth: victory isn't based on how you feel—it's based on what Christ has already done.

The enemy loves to make you feel like you're losing, like the battle is too big, or like you'll never overcome the obstacles in your life. But those are lies. Jesus has already declared victory over every struggle you face. Your feelings may tell you one thing, but God's Word tells you another. When you feel defeated, remind yourself that the battle has already been won—Jesus' victory is your victory.

> Victory doesn't mean you won't face setbacks; it means those setbacks don't define your story.

The enemy might try to trip you up, but he can't change the final outcome. Every struggle is an opportunity to trust in the One who has already overcome. Even when life feels like a losing battle, choose to lean on God's promises, knowing that His strength is made perfect in your weakness. What feels like defeat now is often the soil where God is growing your future victory.

Living as Victorious in Christ

Being victorious in Christ isn't just a future promise—it's a present reality. You don't have to live in defeat or fear. Let's explore how you can live in the victory that Christ has already won for you and walk in that truth daily.

1.   *Discover the Source of Your Victory*

Victory in Christ isn't about mustering up more strength or trying harder—it's about relying on what Jesus has already done. Spend time in prayer and the Word to remind yourself that your victory comes from Christ alone. He has already overcome every obstacle, and you can live confidently in that truth.

2.   *Stand Firm in Your Victory*

Even though Christ has already won the victory, the enemy will still try to deceive you into thinking you're defeated. Stand firm in the truth of your identity as a victorious believer. Don't let the challenges of life shake your faith. When struggles come, declare God's promises over your life and refuse to give in to fear or doubt.

3. *Walk in Daily Victory*

Living in victory isn't just a one-time event—it's a daily choice to trust in Christ's power and promises. Choose to walk in victory every day, whether it's in small battles or big challenges. As you trust in Jesus, you'll experience His strength carrying you through whatever you face.

Discover Who You Are

Prayer

"Lord, thank You for the victory that You've already won through Jesus. I confess that there are times I feel defeated, but I choose to believe that Your victory is my victory. Help me to stand firm in that truth, and remind me that no matter what I face, You have already overcome. Let me live each day in the freedom and confidence of Your victory. In Jesus' name, Amen."

Reflection Questions

1. Are there areas in your life where you feel defeated? How can you remind yourself of Christ's victory in those areas?

2. What does it mean to stand firm in the victory that Jesus has already won for you?

3. How can you walk in victory daily, even in the midst of challenges?

Day 20: Alive in Christ

Memory verse

> "But because of his great love for us, God, who is rich in mercy, made us alive with Christ even when we were dead in transgressions—it is by grace you have been saved."
>
> Ephesians 2:4-5 (NIV)

Before we met Christ, we were spiritually dead. There's no softer way to put it—without Jesus, we were living in darkness, separated from God, and unable to change our own condition. But here's the incredible truth: you are now alive in Christ. What was once dead has been brought to life by the grace of God. You are no longer trapped in sin, no longer separated from God—you are fully alive, spiritually awakened, and made new in Christ.

This transformation isn't just a change in your status—it's a complete resurrection of your identity. The old life, marked by guilt, shame, and spiritual emptiness, has been replaced with a vibrant, abundant life in Jesus. You aren't just breathing; you're thriving, filled with the life that only Christ can give. This new life doesn't depend on your effort or perfection; it's rooted entirely in the finished work of Jesus on the cross.

What does it mean to be fully alive? It means that every part of who you are—your heart, your purpose, your future—has been touched by the power of God's love. You're no longer defined by your past mistakes or the chains that once held you back. Instead, you are free to live in the fullness of Christ's resurrection, with a hope that transforms not only your eternity but also your everyday life.

You Are Alive in Christ

Discover Who You Are

Being alive in Christ means that the old you—the one that was stuck in sin, guilt, and shame—is gone. You've been made new, brought into the fullness of life that only Jesus can give. Ephesians 2:4-5 tells us that even when we were dead in our sins, God, because of His great love for us, made us alive with Christ. This wasn't something we could do on our own—it was the work of God's grace.

What does it mean to be alive in Christ? It means that you've been given a new identity, a new purpose, and a new future. You're no longer bound by the things that once held you captive. You've been resurrected to live a life that reflects the glory of God. And it's not just a future hope—it's a present reality. You are alive right now, living in the power and freedom that comes from knowing Jesus.

Being alive in Christ also means that you're connected to the source of life.

> **Jesus said in John 10:10, "I have come that they may have life, and have it to the full."**

You're not just meant to exist—you're meant to thrive, to experience the abundant, overflowing life that comes from walking with Christ.

I Feel Like I'm in a Dry Season

Sometimes, even though we know we've been made alive in Christ, we don't feel it. We can go through seasons of spiritual dryness or struggle where it feels like that *"alive"* feeling is distant. But here's the thing: your identity as someone who is alive in Christ isn't based on your feelings—it's based on the truth of God's Word.

When you feel spiritually dry, remember that the life Jesus gives you isn't temporary or fleeting. It's permanent. The enemy would love to make you feel like you're still dead in your sins, like the old you is still in control. But the truth is that you've been raised to new life. You're not who you used to be, and the resurrection power of Christ is alive in you, even when you don't feel it.

If you're struggling to feel alive, lean into your relationship with Christ. Spend time in His Word, in prayer, and in worship. Let the truth of His resurrection power stir your heart and awaken your spirit. You are alive, even in the dry seasons.

Living as Someone Alive in Christ

Being alive in Christ isn't just a spiritual truth—it's an identity that shapes how you live every day. You've been raised to new life, given a fresh start, and empowered to live with purpose and joy.

Let's explore how you can walk in the fullness of this new life and live as someone who is fully alive in Christ.

1. Walk in Newness of Life

Being alive in Christ means that the old you is gone. Embrace the new life that Jesus has given you by walking in the freedom, joy, and purpose He provides. Don't let the sins, failures, or regrets of the past define you anymore—you are a new creation, living in the light of Christ's resurrection.

2. Let Christ's Life Flow Through You

Just as a vine gives life to its branches, Jesus gives life to you. Stay connected to Him through prayer, His Word, and fellowship with other believers. Let His life flow through you, shaping your actions, your thoughts, and your relationships. When you stay connected to Christ, His life transforms every part of you.

3. Live Abundantly, Not Just Surviving

Jesus didn't come so that you could just *"get by."* He came to give you life to the full. Live with a sense of abundance, trusting that God has given you everything you need to thrive. This means letting go of a survival mentality and stepping into the overflowing, joy-filled life that God has prepared for you.

Prayer

"Lord, thank You for making me alive in Christ. I confess that there are times I feel spiritually dry or distant, but I choose to believe in the truth of Your Word. Help me to walk in the newness of life You've given me and to live abundantly in Your grace. Let Your resurrection power flow through me and fill every area of my life with joy and purpose. In Jesus' name, Amen."

Reflection Questions

1. Are there areas of your life where you still feel like you're "*surviving*" instead of living fully?

2. How can you embrace the newness of life that Christ has given you, especially in moments of spiritual dryness?

3. What would it look like for you to live in the abundance of Christ's resurrection power daily?

Day 21: Adopted into God's Family

Memory verse

> *"The Spirit you received does not make you slaves, so that you live in fear again; rather, the Spirit you received brought about your adoption to son ship. And by him we cry, 'Abba, Father.'"*
>
> Romans 8:15 (NIV)

Discover Who You Are

Adoption is one of the most powerful images the Bible uses to describe our relationship with God. When you think of adoption, you might picture a child being welcomed into a loving family, given a new name, and receiving the full rights of that family. That's exactly what happened to you in Christ.

> You were not just saved from your sins—you were brought into the family of God, with all the rights and privileges of a beloved child.

This isn't just a legal transaction; it's a heart transaction. God didn't just sign the adoption papers—He wrote your name on His heart. He brought you into His family not out of obligation but out of His overwhelming love. When God calls you His child, it's not just a title—it's an eternal declaration that you belong, that you're wanted, and that you're cherished. You are part of a family where love is unconditional, acceptance is unshakable, and your place is secure.

You are not a distant servant or someone barely tolerated—you are God's child, adopted into His family through Jesus. This is your identity: loved, chosen, and accepted by your Heavenly Father.

You Are Adopted into God's Family

In Roman culture, adoption was a serious legal process. When a child was adopted, they received a new identity, the family's name, and full inheritance rights. The same is true for us spiritually. Romans 8:15 tells us that through the Spirit, we have been adopted into God's family, and we have the right to call Him *"Abba, Father"*—a term of intimacy, closeness, and trust.

> You didn't earn your place in God's family—it was given to you freely through Jesus.

You've been brought out of spiritual orphan hood and placed into a family where you are loved unconditionally. And this adoption isn't temporary—it's eternal. God will never abandon you or revoke your status as His child. You are fully accepted, loved, and cherished by your Heavenly Father.

As a child of God, you also have access to the inheritance of His Kingdom. You are not a stranger or outsider; you are part of the family. Your identity as a son or daughter of God means that you are secure, valued, and chosen for a life of purpose in His Kingdom.

I Don't Feel Like I Belong

At times, it's easy to feel like we don't fully belong—whether that's in our families, our communities, or even in God's family. Maybe you've felt like your past disqualifies you from being fully accepted by God, or maybe you've struggled with the idea that God could truly love and value you as His own. But here's the truth: your adoption into God's family isn't based on your performance—it's based on His grace.

The enemy loves to make you feel like you're not truly part of God's family, whispering lies that you're not good enough or that you're still an outsider. But those are just that—lies. God has chosen you and welcomed you into His family with open arms. You are not a second-class citizen in the Kingdom of God—you are a beloved child, fully embraced by your Heavenly Father.

When doubts creep in, remind yourself of this truth: God doesn't adopt halfway. In Roman culture, adoption was irrevocable—the adopted child became a permanent member of the family with full rights and privileges. How much more secure is our place in God's family, sealed by the blood of Christ? God's love for you is unchanging and eternal, and your identity as His child is unshakable.

> You belong—not because of who you are, but because of whose you are.

Living as Someone Adopted into God's Family

Being adopted into God's family means that you are not only saved but also fully embraced as a beloved child of God. Let's explore how you can live confidently in this identity and experience the fullness of being part of God's family.

1. Embrace Your Identity as a Child of God

Your identity as an adopted child of God means that you are deeply loved and fully accepted.

> Stop living like you have to earn God's approval or love—you already have it.

Embrace the truth that you are His child, and live in the confidence that comes from knowing your Father loves you unconditionally.

2. Cry Out to Your Father

One of the privileges of being adopted into God's family is the ability to approach Him with boldness and intimacy. You can cry out to Him as "*Abba, Father*," knowing that He hears you and cares for you. When you're in need, in pain, or in doubt, turn to God as your loving Father who wants to be close to you.

3. Live Secure in God's Family

As a child of God, you have a secure place in His family—nothing can take that away. Let go of the fear of rejection or abandonment and rest in the assurance that God's love for you is unchanging. You are safe in His family, and nothing can separate you from His love.

Prayer

"Lord, thank You for adopting me into Your family. I confess that there are times I struggle to believe I am fully accepted by You, but today I choose to embrace my identity as Your beloved child. Help me to live in the confidence of Your love, and let me cry out to You as my Father, knowing that You care for me deeply. Thank You for making me part of Your family. In Jesus' name, Amen."

Reflection Questions

1. Are there areas in your life where you struggle to believe that you are fully accepted and loved by God as His child?

2. How can you live with greater confidence in your identity as a son or daughter of God?

3. What would change in your relationship with God if you truly embraced Him as your loving Father?

More Books by Jason Hanash

Latest Release
The Spiritual Battlefield

The Spiritual Battlefield unveils the three critical arenas where these conflicts take place: the demonic, the flesh, and the world. With clarity and depth, you will be guided through each of these battlegrounds, providing biblical insights and practical strategies to conquer the forces that seek to ensnare and defeat you.

Buy Now

Freedom

If you are brave enough to identify and inspect the chains that are keeping you in bondage, take captive the lies of the enemy, and allow God to heal and transform you into a new creation—you can experience FREEDOM.

Buy Now

Discover Who You Are

Man Up

Too many people today are confused about masculinity and manhood, caught up in popular misunderstandings and deceptions. Our culture has reframed identity and gender, including masculinity, to the point that even believers have a tough time comprehending what it means to be a man, especially a man following Jesus.

Buy Now

CONNECT WITH JASON HANASH ONLINE AT

WWW.JASONHANASH.COM

@PASTORJASONHANASH

@JASON HANASH

@PASTORJASONHANASH

Made in the USA
Middletown, DE
10 January 2025